Destined To Win Volume 7

She Speaks: A Compilation of Women in Ministry

Copyright © Tammy Vaughan

ISBN: 978-1-958186-37-4

LOC: ACCEPTED

Publisher and Editor:

The FYreHouse Multimedia Enterprises, LLC

Fiery Beacon Publishing House, LLC

Fiery Beacon Consulting and Publishing Group

This work was produced in Greensboro, North Carolina, United States of America. All rights reserved under International Copyright Law. The contents of this work are not necessarily the views of Fiery Beacon Publishing House, LLC, nor any of its affiliates. No portion of this publication may be reproduced, stored in any electronic system, or transmitted in any form or by any means (electronic, mechanical, photocopy, recording, or otherwise) without written permission from Tammy Vaughan and The FYreHouse Multimedia Enterprises, LLC. Brief quotations may be used in literary reviews. Unless otherwise noted, all scripture references have been presented from the New King James or Amplified versions of the Bible. All definitions in this work have been presented by Google Dictionary(copyright.)

Destined to Win

Volume 7

She Speaks: A Compilation of
Women in Ministry

A Literary Vision by

Tammy Vaughan

Table of Contents

Introduction   "From My Heart to Yours"

Acknowledgements

The Author's Declaration

A Prayer for You and Your Reading Journey

Literary Voices

Pastor Carolyn Williams Gorham

"Life After the Fall"   11

Pastor Chantal Zoe Amis

"I Got My Voice Back! RoaRRRrrr!!!"   29

Minister Connie Bridges

"Looking for Validation in All the Wrong Places"   45

Elder Natalie Scott

"From Barren to Birthing"   57

Pastor Priscilla Williams

"The Divine Sacrifice"   73

Rev. Dr. Rhonda Royal Hatton

Destined to Walk in my Calling:

Talitha Cumi! Girl, Get UP!   95

Apostle Sharon Cotton

"Yes, it Hurt, But GOD!"   107

Pastor Tammy Vaughan

"Called, Equipped and Empowered:

A Journey of a Woman in Ministry"   123

From My Heart to Yours....

Dear Sister,

If no one has told you lately, you are doing holy work. Heaven sees your sacrifice. God delights in your "yes." You are a modern-day Deborah, a faithful Mary, a courageous Esther, a prophetic. You carry the fragrance of Christ and the fire of the Holy Spirit.

When doors close, remember that God opens better ones. When you feel unseen, know that God is spotlighting you in the Spirit.
When tears fall, God is bottling everyone.

Keep preaching. Keep praying. Keep planting. Keep pressing.
There's a generation waiting for your obedience.

"Blessed is she who believed that the Lord would fulfill His promises to her" (Luke 1:45).

You are called.
You are equipped.
You are empowered.

Keep going. The world needs your voice, your wisdom, your witness.

With love and sisterhood,
Pastor Tammy

Acknowledgments

With heartfelt gratitude, we dedicate this anthology to every woman who has answered the call to ministry. Your voices, stories, and testimonies are sacred and powerful. Thank you for your courage to speak, your willingness to serve, and your faith to lead.

To our contributing authors—thank you for your transparency, wisdom, and obedience. Each chapter reflects a unique journey marked by God's grace, and together they form a tapestry of inspiration and truth. Your words will uplift, challenge, and empower readers for years to come.

Special thanks to the editors, prayer partners, and supporters who helped bring this vision to life. Your behind-the-scenes labor has not gone unnoticed, and we are deeply grateful.

Most importantly, we acknowledge our Sovereign God—who calls, equips, and sustains. May this collection glorify Him and encourage women across the globe to boldly pursue their divine assignment.

The Author's Declaration

We decree and declare that we can do all things through Christ Jesus who strengthens us. We are thankful for the tests and trials that led us to this point. We walk in the spirit of truth and believe there is healing in our stories. We decree and declare that as we tell our stories and use it as a reminder that God takes what has been "Crushed" and allows it to "Survive" we decree and declare that we will never be defeated. We stand in the positional truth that we are in a victorious fight against the devil. We declare that we will not be silent. We WIN…because We are DESTINED TO WIN!

~ **Co-Author Nakenya Arthur**

My Prayer for You and Your Reading Journey

Father God,

I come to You as humbly as I know how, thanking You for the precious soul preparing to read this book. I ask that You open their heart and spirit to receive every word with clarity and purpose. May each page mark the beginning of a healing journey—spiritually, personally, and mentally.

Lord, I pray that each chapter ministers deeply, bringing comfort, revelation, and strength. Let Your presence be felt with every turn of the page, reminding the reader that they are not alone. May this book be a vessel through which You speak, heal, and restore.

Most of all, Father, I pray that through this book, the reader is drawn closer to becoming all You've created them to be. I thank You in advance for the transformation, breakthroughs, and peace that will manifest through this work.

I ask all these things in the mighty name of Jesus. Amen.

~ **Pastor Tammy**

Carolyn Gorham

Pastor Carolyn Gorham is a devoted servant of God, a visionary leader, and a passionate advocate for women's ministry. As a wife, mother, pastor, and non-profit founder, she gracefully weaves together faith, family, and purpose, inspiring countless lives along the way.

Born with a keen intellect and a heart for service, Pastor Carolyn pursued a degree in Computer Programming. Yet, while her technical skills flourished, her deepest joy was found in the art of photography—a passion that allows her to capture the beauty of God's creation and the stories of His people. She is a graduate of Higher Learning Bible Institute and is currently enrolled in New Life School of Theology. She is the Senior Pastor of Word Empowerment (WE) Church Wilson in Wilson, NC, under the direction of Apostle Dr. J. Lemuel Spence.

In addition to her pastoral role, Pastor Carolyn is the founder and director of Loving Hand Outreach Ministries. For the past thirteen years, she and her staff have supported youth and families through impactful programs and outreach.

Guided by Matthew 22:37-40, Pastor Carolyn remains committed to the calling God has placed upon her life – to serve and to lead. Whether through a sermon, a heartfelt prayer, or the lens of her camera, she continues to capture and share the beauty of God's love.

Contact Pastor Carolyn:

Email: carolyngorhamministries@gmail.com

Facebook: https://www.facebook.com/carolyn.w.gorham

Instagram: www.instagram.com/mrscgorham

Life After the Fall

By Pastor Carolyn Gorham

I FELL HARD!

Imagine going to a church service and deviating from the way you usually enter the edifice and the styles of shoes you are accustomed to wearing. My daughter noted that I usually enter from the far rear, but I chose a different route. As we were walking, I stumbled and struggled to catch and maintain my balance; however, it was to no avail. I braced for impact, and I slid and rolled. I was bloody, bruised, and sore. The palms of my hands had pebbles and gravel in them. My knee was scraped to the white meat, and you could see the blood mingled with the debris of the concrete. My body felt the impact. As my daughter checked on me, others who witnessed the fall were on their way to my rescue.

How many times have we deviated from our "normal" course and found ourselves in a different predicament had we stayed the course and played it safe? Please don't misunderstand what I'm saying. Change is good and is often necessary. If we are honest, it is easy to become creatures of habit; thus, there is a need to change our routine sometimes. Some have fallen privately, and some more publicly than others. Even in what man may deem a hard fall, God sees an opportunity for you to draw closer to Him. The Oxford Language defines fall,

"As moving downward, typically rapidly and freely without control, from a higher to a lower level, as well as (a person) losing one's balance and collapse."

Just as a baby begins to walk independently, they stumble and fall. The parents watch excitedly to see how they will handle the fall – will they give up or try again? Then, the parents encourage them to get up and walk again. It graduates to fall when they're learning how to ride a bicycle without the training wheels or navigating a skateboard. Eventually, they become resilient enough to bounce back on their own, and the parents become a little anxious because the children realize it's not that bad and that they're ready to try the next stunt. In life, you are going to fall, make mistakes, and, some would even say, fail. It is all in your perspective.

When I look back on my life, I realize that during the moments I fell - I felt defeated, overcome by doubt, or too weary to move forward - God always placed someone in my path to uplift and encourage me. Whether through a kind word, a helping hand, or simply their presence, He reminded me that I was never alone. In my weakest moments, His grace reached me through others, renewing my strength and giving me the courage to keep going.

I am Carolyn Gorham, wife, mother, and friend. I have served the church in various capacities since 1995/1996. I am the Founder and Director of Loving Hand Outreach Ministries and the newly appointed pastor of WE Church Wilson. I did not come from a deeply religious, churchgoing family that attended church every Sunday and throughout the week. However, I attended church with my grandmother occasionally for funerals and gospel singing. My mother never stopped me from going to church with my friends. I would walk to choir rehearsal with my neighbors and hang out afterward. There was an indescribable feeling about those times at church that gave me peace. A few years later, my Christian journey began in my freshman year of high school at the church where I went with my friends for choir rehearsal. Plenty of churches were around, but there was something about that place. That is where I felt a connection. I could sit there long after the activities were finished. I would sit in the back row during the church meetings, not understanding any of the business being discussed, but because it was in the weekly announcements, I showed up and watched.

On Sundays, I went to church by walking, catching a cab, or having my mom drop me off. My mom would drop me off for Bible study, and one of the deacons would take me home. It was during the drives home that he shared the Word, his faith, and his testimonies and encouraged me. I must tell you the love and admiration I have for the Deacon and his wife, who was a mother in the church, is indescribable. They were terrific examples of servants of the Lord. He and his wife were truly God-sent.

However, despite my efforts to be good and not attend parties (I told my mom when I got saved, "Don't let me go to no parties no matter how hard I try to go), guess what? I fell! I wanted to have fun. I eventually stopped attending church and would duck when I saw the Deacon from time to time when I would pick my brother up from school. I remember reclining my seat and turning my head so the

Deacon would not see me despite him being parked beside my mother's vehicle. I couldn't deny seeing him. The Deacon told me he would ask my brother about me occasionally. I can truly say he never treated me any differently than the times before, and he didn't pressure me to come back to the church. He reminded me of God's love for me. The deacon even introduced me to the new Pastor and his wife one Sunday afternoon in a local restaurant.

Years later, I recalled when I told my brother to ask Deacon what I needed to do to return to the church. On Wednesday, November 30, 1994, my daughter and I went to church and sat on the second pew on the left side of the church during Bible Study. With my face drenched in tears, snotty nose, and longing for God, I re-dedicated my life to the Lord in the Pastor's Study surrounded by some older saints. My life has never been the same. I get joy when I think about where God has brought me from and all He has done for me. From sleeping in the house with a pot of boiling water on the stove and a gun to protect my family to being ambushed with a car full of people, being chased the wrong way down one-way streets, driving down the highway with a gun pulled on us on a Halloween night with my one-year-old daughter in the back seat, to declaring that God is my shelter, my rock, and my protector.

When I received the call into ministry in 1998, I did not go running because I was content serving and singing in the choir. I questioned God. I wanted to make sure it was not me; I was not imagining it, in addition to the fight of people's views of women in ministry, including my grandmothers' thoughts. I was like Gideon, asking for more signs and getting them. I finally said, "God, if this is what you are calling me to, let somebody who doesn't know me come to me." I arrived at work early one morning thinking I would be alone. While in my cubicle, an older lady came and began to confirm what God had said. I called my Bishop to have a face-to-face with him. The weight that fell off when I said "Yes" was unsurmountable.

I preached my initial sermon on Sunday, January 3, 1999, entitled "Who Did Hinder You?" from Galatians 5:7 under the guidance of Bishop Robert L. Gorham at Wilson Chapel Free Will Baptist Church (formerly Wilson Chapel UAFWB). I had family who disagreed, and I was okay with that. I have learned that there is more for you than against you. The challenges I encountered while serving my spouse, two beautiful children, family, work, ministry, and community were sometimes daunting and understated. However, the grace of God avails, and Holy Spirit often gives strategies to perform effortlessly. But let us talk about the pain of ministry.

As much as I thought serving in ministry was glorious and wonderful, I also experienced the gut-wrenching pain of being talked about by those who labored with me, having my kids talked about and ostracized because of who their mother was. The very thing that I ran from was what God used to mature me. I ran from the pain. I did not want to experience the pain of separation and rejection riddled with disappointment and betrayal. I backed away from the participation of events, the self-isolation, the distancing of myself from others. The pain would not let me out of its grip, but guess what? Pain is inexorable and necessary for growth.

My maturity has taught me some of my expectations of the church caused the pain to feel worse than it was! I thought the church was a group of "perfect" people, that forgave, loved, and were happy. What I found out is, the "church" is comprised of different types of people, looking for different things, and some are saved by a forgiving and gracious God, and are works in progress. They are a group of imperfect people growing in grace.

Psalm 119:71(AMP) is a good reference point. In the pain, I sought God's face even more. The psalmist wrote,

> **"It is good for me that I have been afflicted; that I might learn thy statutes."**

The ISV interpretation reads,

> **"It was for my good that I was humbled; so that I would learn your statutes."**

At the deepest depths of your pain, you must press your way. You must encourage yourself and remind yourself there is glory after this. There is restoration after this. There is healing after this. Many nights, I asked God to take the pain away. I just wanted it to end. Amid my crying out, I had to fight. I had to fight the enemy, I had to fight wrong mindsets, and I had to pull down strongholds. The Apostle Paul describes it best in 2 Corinthians 10: 4-6 (NKJV):

> **"4) For the weapons of our warfare are not carnal but mighty in God for pulling down strongholds, 5) casting down arguments and every high thing that exalts itself against the knowledge of God, bringing every thought into captivity to the obedience of Christ, 6) and being**

ready to punish all disobedience when your obedience is fulfilled."

I served in my home church until 2016. I went to support my sister-in-love's first church service in the sanctuary on January 3, 2016, and I stayed until October 2021. Through much prayer, fasting and tears I sought the Lord, and my Bishop gave his blessings and released me to serve. It was under her leadership I served as Assistant Pastor, Pastor and received prophetic training. There were obstacles to overcome, challenges to champion and much growth took place. I will remember "You can't conquer what you won't confront". Confrontation is not always negative and is sometimes needed.

HAVE YOU DEALT WITH YOU?

The question was asked, "Have you dealt with you?" I thought I had, but truth be told, I had not. What I did was suppressed and moved. When I finally settled down and looked in the mirror, I had to accept the harsh reality I had not dealt with me. I brushed over some areas because I did not want to deal with them. I wanted God to remove them from my memory like it never happened. I did not want to confront the pain. I did not want to peel the scab.

I had to confront myself. I had to confront the fact that I became a people-pleaser in the name of "just to get along" and keeping the peace. I found myself in survival mode. I had moments of happiness, but I was not happy.

I had to confront the fact that I was different and find my niche. Even as a child, I did not fit in certain circles, and I had to be okay with that. Understanding who God created you to be is critical. I had to confront the fact that I placed myself in a box, not others. Other people's words wounded me because I had not dealt with the spirit of rejection. Everything said to me was not out of malicious intent but for maturation purposes. To move from milk to meat.

We are all uniquely created by God's design. David declared in Psalms 139:14,

> **"I will praise you, for I am fearfully and wonderfully made; Marvelous are your works, And that my soul knows very well."**

We are intricately woven in God's image. According to Luke 12:7, **"God knows how many hairs you have on your head..."** Moreover, Ephesians 2:10 in the Amplified Bible states,

> **"For we are His workmanship [His own master work, a work of art], created in Christ Jesus [reborn from above—spiritually transformed, renewed, ready to be used] for good works, which God prepared [for us] beforehand [taking paths which He set], so that we would walk in them [living the good life which He prearranged and made ready for us]."**

I had to take a step back and assess the situation, take inventory of my thoughts, put words to my feelings and my actions, confront the ugly truths of myself, and give them to God. I had to repent. I lamented over what was and what could have been while accepting the reality of what is. I was dealing with my humanity while navigating the call upon my life. I wanted to sit down and return to the basics. I did not want to go forth, but that would have been a great injustice and a disservice to mankind. I realized I am a spirit being with an earthly body and earthly emotions but possessing divine connections. No matter how much I tried to hide, I could not deny the call of God on my life.

HE LED ME HERE

As I sought God's direction for my life, I was in an unknown space. I had to trust God, work through those feelings, traumas, and issues I suppressed, and allow God to heal me from the inside out. Healing can come in different forms and spaces: Godly counsel, therapists, and small groups. I had various outlets and other circles.

While preparing for church, I heard about Lady Suzette Spence's testimony from Durham, N.C. I contemplated hard because I wanted to listen to her, but I did not want to make that hour-and-a-half drive. I opted for a church about twenty-five minutes from my home, and I can honestly say God is in control, and the Lord orders my steps. Lady Suzette Spence was the guest preacher, and she preached **"He Led Me Here."**

At that moment, I knew the Lord was orchestrating my steps. I started traveling the three-hour round trip journey every

Sunday. I used to think people were insane driving long distances for church, but God knows what is needed and when. As women in ministry, it is imperative to get out of your own way and start making connections. It may look strange to some, but it does not have to be explained when God begins to reveal Himself to you. Modern technology offers many ways to connect, but human connection is unmatched. God continues to bless me with excellent sisters and brothers on this journey who pray with me, cover me, speak life, and tell me the truth. They hold me accountable and do not let me wallow in self-pity. Galatians 6:1 (KJV),

"Brethren, if a man be overtaken in a fault, ye which are spiritual, restore such a one in the spirit of meekness; considering thyself, lest thou also be tempted."

Your circles may change as you grow and mature, as you come to the fruition of who you are but learn to speak kindly to others and yourself. No one's fall is the same. **In 1 Peter 4:8, we are admonished,**

"And above all, we have fervent love for one another, for love will cover a multitude of sins."

Women of God do not do ministry for the sake of doing ministry. Remember the call and remember the why. Let me encourage you on your journey. No matter how many times you fall, **"Rise, take up thy bed, and walk!"** (John 5:8 KJV) By design, we have free will, and it is up to you to have faith in God. Proverbs 16:9, **"In their hearts, humans plan their course, but the LORD establishes their steps."**

Like other historical figures of the Bible, those in our lifetime and before have fallen, and you too may fall. When you do, get up; if you need help, it's okay. Do not let pride overtake you. Those close to you may not have the strength or be able to help you, but there'll be somebody at the right time who will help you up, help you walk, clean your bruises, bandage you, and aid in your healing. The pain you feel when you fall serves a purpose, and the pain you feel because of the fall has a purpose. I trust that you are going to get through it because someone is going to need your testimony. Revelations 12:11 states, **"We overcome by the word of our testimony and the blood of the Lamb."** You may have done things you thought were so bad that God wouldn't forgive you, but God is a loving Father. 1 John 1:9 states,

"If we confess our sins, he is faithful and just and will forgive us our sins and purify us from all unrighteousness."

Don't allow shame and guilt to overtake you.

You are more than a conqueror.

The Bible declares in Proverbs 24:16, **"For a righteous person falls seven times, but he gets up again..."** Regardless of how often you fall, you must remember God's eyes are upon you. He calculated everything you've done before time. Show yourself grace! You may have prided yourself on being able to stand and be faithful, but the unthinkable happened: you fell. How often have you said, "I would NEVER," but did? Can you imagine how Peter felt after Jesus foretold his denial and it came to pass? How did his ego suffer after making bold declarations? Did he forget in such a short time who Jesus was and that He spoke the truth? During the Last Supper, after Jesus apprised the disciples in Matthew 26:31, "All ye shall be offended because of me this night..." but Peter boldly declared in his arrogance in verse 33, "Though all men shall be offended because of thee, yet will I <u>never</u> be offended."

In verse 34, Jesus warned Peter, **"Verily I say unto thee, that this night, before the cock crow, thou shalt deny me thrice."** Who disputes the Master? Who tells the Master, "You don't know what you're talking about"? Peter tries to persuade Jesus (v. 35), "Though I should die with thee, yet will I not deny thee." He esteemed himself higher than he should have esteemed himself.

What happened? Peter denied knowing Jesus during the trial in Matthew 26:69 –70 when the damsel pointed out he was with Jesus of Galilee; in verses 71-72, when he was on the porch, and another maid saw him and told him he was with Jesus of Galilee; and in verses 73-74 when others told Peter he was one of them because of his speech. Immediately after Peter denied knowing Jesus the third time, the cock crew.

"And Peter remembered the word of Jesus, which said unto him, Before the cock crow, thou shalt deny me thrice. And he went out and wept bitterly."

(Matthew 26:75)

Let me encourage you. Do not count yourself out. Examine your motives and repent. Forgive yourself. God has not counted you out. God restored Peter. After the fall, Peter's life changed. He recommitted himself, dealt with himself, and grew. When Peter preached at Jerusalem,

> "...they that gladly received his word were baptized: and the same day there were added unto them about three thousand souls."
>
> (Acts 2:41)

Life after the fall is more wonderful than I could have imagined. I did not die in it. I got up, took up my bed, and I am walking!! What I thought was the end, was just another beginning. I had to remind myself of who I was through God's Word:

WORDS OF AFFIRMATION

"I am loved." **1 John 4:19**

"I am chosen." **Ephesians 1:4-5**

"I am chosen and ordained to bear fruit that will last." **John 15:16**

"I am sealed with the Holy Spirit of promise." **Ephesians 1:13**

"I am enslaved to God." **Romans 6:22**

"I am forgiven." **1 John 1:9**

"I am fearfully and wonderfully made." **Psalm 139:14**

"I am the salt of the earth." **Matthew 5:13**

"I am free from condemnation." **John 5:24**

"I am complete in Him." **Colossians 2:10**

"I am in Christ Jesus by His doing." **1 Corinthians 1:30**

"I am washed, sanctified, and justified in the name of the Lord Jesus and by the Spirit of our God." **1 Corinthians 6:11**

"My body is the temple of the Holy Spirit, who is in me, whom I received from God. I am not my own; I was bought with a price." **1 Corinthians 6:19-20**

"I am reconciled to God." **2 Corinthians 5:18**

"I am the righteousness of God in Christ Jesus." **2 Corinthians 5:21**

"I submit myself to God who gives more grace to the humble, and He will lift me up."

1 Peter 5:6

"I am the head and not the tail, above and not beneath." **Deuteronomy 28:13**

"I am the elect of God." **Colossians 3:12**

"I am strong in the Lord." **Ephesians 6:10**

"I am more than a conqueror." **Romans 8:37**

"I am joint heir with Christ." **Romans 8:13**

A Place of Divine Reflection

A Place of Divine Reflection

Chantale Z Amis

Chantale Zoe Amis is known by her first and middle name, Zoe - both names that the Lord instructed through her father. It means to boldly declare "the God-kind of life". Chantale was born in Queens, NY, and was raised in Sussex County, New Jersey. She made her way down to Phili, majoring in Graphic Design at The Art Institute of Philadelphia. She is a wife, mother of two, and has the honor of serving at Next Dimension Family Church in Burlington, NJ, and is currently training to become a licensed minister.

Chantale is an artist and the CEO of Zoe Experience, bringing brands and graphics to life and creating prophetic paintings. Other than working with her hands, she has a burden to see God's people live life free. She takes great joy in helping others through prayer, ministering the Word, or mentorship. She has a soft spot, in particular, for women. Having been a single mother after college, she is well aware of the struggle the world tries to trap us in. She desires for all women to see the hidden gems on the inside of them, learning to operate boldly with the image of Christ in us. As an artist and an entrepreneur who has been blessed with many creative gifts, she aims to please the Lord by stewarding them to reveal His glory.

<u>**Contact Chantale:**</u>

Email: create@zoeexperience.com

Facebook: https://www.facebook.com/chantale.zoe.amis

Instagram: www.instagram.com/zoe.experience

www.zoeexperience.com

I GOT MY VOICE BACK: ROARRRrrr!

By Chantale Zoe Amis

Do you remember the first time you heard your voice in a video or voicemail and as soon as you heard it, you immediately said, "Wait, that's what my voice sounds like?" Then you paused and adjusted with what you just heard in your ear to your outer ear, or didn't like it all. I have found that many people don't take the time to listen to the beauty within hearing their own voice; there is something that is being exposed that is unfamiliar, a new perspective of *how others hear you.*

This is somewhat of what my life has been like, seeing two different versions of yourself. You see, I like what my voice sounds like, I don't cringe, as some might. The truth is, for most of my life I was made to feel or was told that my voice didn't matter. Now, that wasn't stated in those exact words, but it was certainly communicated through people's actions and the thoughts that came after being misunderstood. It felt as if I never had the right way or timing to say something, or that I had too much say. But I liked speaking, so this was difficult for me for so many reasons. I'm sure many people can resonate with this feeling and frustration, whether it is from your childhood to adult relationships, work environments, church settings, etc.

Over time, I have found that if you don't realize where your real voice comes from, and why you have experienced feeling or being muzzled, you can eventually be that way with God. If I'm not confident with my voice, how can I speak to Him when my flesh is already weak? *Matthew 26:41 says,*

"The spirit is willing, but the flesh is weak."

The more time I spent with the Lord, I discovered a growl in my belly, a "roar," so to say. The more I opened my mouth, adversity hit, again and again. I would eventually emotionally withdraw because that was way too uncomfortable for me. There would be so much beauty, and then boom, the warfare would come. Thoughts of staying under the covers so I didn't have to face it would come in like a flood. Whether it was physical covers or covering myself with comfort, it brought me back to the feelings of being a little girl. A ball of fire would form in my throat, but it would feel like nothing could come out until roarrr, emotions hit. This roar was filled with frustration and was undisciplined. At the core, I wanted to be heard but didn't want to disappoint the person I was confronted with. Why? Because I'm someone who wants to love everyone and everyone to love each other. This unfortunately is how people-pleasing sprung up. Isn't love meant to be non-confrontational, where you can find a middle ground so that everyone can be happy, right? Over time, I noticed I was making my voice and myself smaller and smaller. But what about the *roa*r, the one I found in my time with God? It was loud, uncomfortable, and beautiful all at the same time. Here are the two versions of me again: the girl who didn't want to say the wrong thing and the other, a boss, who had no fear at all.

Even though I knew that the adversary comes to kill, steal, and destroy (John 10:10), I didn't violently take what was mine because I was only looking at *my* image. I didn't know how to use this new roar that I found while with God because, well, it was quite consuming. I allowed fear to consume me more than I realized and it was another hindrance to speaking to the Father. My prayer and study time would be less consistent due to what was attached to it for me, the one who came *like* a roaring lion. But I didn't realize my roar, the one filled with the Holy Ghost, could pummel those lies in a heartbeat. My spiritual backbone needed strengthening, my inner man, but the more I tried to strengthen my spirit man by killing my flesh, it rebelled by retreating, again. All the while my mind and heart would be on the Lord, but I would find it hard to see myself in the way His Word was showing. I kept seeing myself as not enough, even though I saw the lioness in me and heard it, I wavered. I became exhausted and wanted this cycle to stop but I had to face what I didn't want to.

James 1:2-3 says,

> **"Consider it pure joy, my brothers and sisters, whenever you face trials of many kinds, because you know that the testing of your faith produces perseverance."**

As you can see, I didn't want to face any trials, let alone *many* trials, and then to be tested on top of that, but I knew I had to. This was a necessary process for The GREATER One to rise in me. I'm not talking about *my* voice anymore, but *His*, and that's what I was missing in all of it. For the Greater Voice in me to rise, I had to kill all the other voices with the all-consuming Voice. I don't face trials by myself but with His Word. It's sharper than any two-edged sword! So, when the lie that I was a failure, or wasn't enough arose, I would shout "LIES!!" I would declare that me by myself is not enough, and doing it in my understanding won't be enough, and I would thank God for His Truth freeing me. God saw us as valuable vessels to live in us and make us in His image and likeness. I once heard this saying, "I'm a King's kid", and I would picture all the benefits that come with being an earthly prince or princess. All they have to do is say "My father, the king, granted such and such" and they have the proof of their crown or crest as a Royal Prince or Princess. Embracing this royal crown is how we will be transformed (Romans 12:2). What crown are you wearing? Is it a crown that is broken, dirty, or flimsy like a costume's crown? Is it a counterfeit, or is it pure gold, filled with gems and rubies that's so heavy to wear and gives you authority to say, and it shall be?

One of the most influential voices in my life was my father's voice (and still is 13 years after he passed). The times that the emotional roar came out of me when I felt like he didn't understand me, or when I was telling my dad how I felt misunderstood by someone, he would say,

"Chantale, the Bible tells us to be slow to speak, and quick to hear." (James 1:19)

He would say it so gently, but it sounded like Chinese at the time. He was correcting me in love and showing me a better way. I'm so glad he planted that seed in me so that I can look back many years later and see how far I have grown in this truth. James 1:20 says,

> "...for the anger of man does not produce the righteousness of God."

These two verses are a command for us to understand and a warning of where it can take us if we don't. Just two verses later, it says to be a doer of the Word. We know that faith comes by hearing, and we also know that out of the abundance of the heart, the mouth speaks. What we say out loud shows us what we are hearing, and what's abiding in our hearts. So many of our frustrations grow because we're not asking for *His* voice to rise in us, and that's the confidence we are supposed to remain in.

After all, talking a lot has opened many great doors for me, including allowing me to help women and men of all ages, nationally and internationally by administering The Word, and now writing for this book. What the enemy used to make me feel lesser, was all because he knew I *did* have something to say…BUT GOD. Though the adversity can be rough, at the same time, it can teach you what to stand for and how. I like to say, the enemy tells on himself all the time. But if we aren't slow to speak, or transformed, we're going to miss out on the fact that he's actually confirming what God called us to be great in. I'm so thankful that God's Word will do what it was sent to do, never allowing me to give up and throw in the towel. As I dove into the Word of Life more, in study, meditation, and prayer, I found that roar not only getting louder but now being fruitful in my life and over the lives of others. I found a new strength and resilience in it all. But I must abide in Him because my voice is nothing without His. Yes, I may like the sound of my voice, but it's His Word that allows my voice to make the sound that reveals His Glory, the voice that could move mountains as I believe in Him.

The Word of God is like a mirror and will show us ourselves, and thankfully so, but when you are in His word, you will see His reflection, since He is *the Word,* remember that. While walking in His Word, you should look and sound like the Word, it shall speak for you.

"For if anyone is a hearer of the word and not a doer, he is like a man observing his natural face in a mirror; for he observes himself, goes away, and immediately forgets what kind of man he was."

James 1:23-24

So, the question is, how do I get and sustain this confident voice that isn't mine, but is within me? Can you guess? It's in abiding. John 15:7 states,

"If you abide in Me, and My words abide in you, you will ask what you desire, and it shall be done for you. [8] By this My Father is glorified, that you bear much fruit; so, you will be My disciples."

There are so many benefits to abiding in Him, which is why the enemy tries to run us off! Jesus said in John 5:19-20, *"...Very truly I tell you, the Son can do nothing by Himself; He can do only what He sees His Father doing, because whatever the Father does the Son also does. [20] For the Father loves the Son and shows Him all He does. Yes, and He will show Him even greater works than these, so that you will be amazed."* If Jesus only said what He heard the Father say, then what makes us think we can do differently? We have an invitation to *abide* with the One who loves us, but we must violently take this invitation by force. Even now as I write, the enemy is trying to flood my mind with thoughts that I don't have enough time and that I don't know what else to say. Remember the one who told *me* that I talked too much? So, I violently clap back by pushing the buttons on the keyboard while seeking to hear God's voice to combat the lie on the other side.

Can you imagine if Eve roared? Funny to picture, right? Roaring back at a serpent, but as a human? But that's what the authority of God does. It can make us look funny in the natural. His word gives us dominion over the creeping things, and the serpent certainly crept into that tree. Picture this: someone roaring without confidence and someone roaring with confidence. One will sound like a copycat, and the other will shake you on your insides and can be heard far and wide. Sometimes we say back to the enemy what we *believe* God said, but we don't fully understand so instead, we sound like a cat instead of a lion, or we look like a small candle instead of a burning bush. The outcome of this shaky roar can create a gap in our minds from the Truth, and in turn, we end up submitting to the enemy instead of submitting to God so that we can *resist the enemy*. Standing and speaking in authority takes discipline, and that discipline leads us to see how else we can look like the Master.

I found that being misunderstood paved a path for me to seek the Lord even more, but it took me looking deep within to see why it was happening. The next important step was to find out what I was to do as I was healing and walking in His Word. I knew He was calling me higher and that meant I had to lessen myself, my ways, and my understanding. As you follow Him, there will be times that you just might look a little crazy, but as you humble yourself His Word will defend and speak for you. As you obey His word, that Word shall come to pass. I encourage you to hold fast until you see it because it *will* be worth it.

I ask you this: What is consuming you? What are you saying? What are you thinking and where are you abiding? We know the importance of thinking about good things, even the world knows that, but are we speaking the good things that our Good Father has told us? We are commanded this in Joshua 1:8, *"This Book of the Law shall not depart from your mouth, but you shall meditate on it day and night, so that you may be careful to do according to all that is written in it. For then you will make your way prosperous, and then you will have good success."* The key to experiencing, believing, and communicating God's will is found in saying what He said. It sounds easy, right? As humans, we can easily be consumed with ways and words that are not God's. But it is His breath that consumes the lies because all Scripture is God-breathed. We must posture ourselves to open our mouths so that *He* may fill it (Psalm 81:10). That is what God told the Israelites to do when He took them out of Egypt, but when they opened up their mouths all they did was complain because they wanted the familiar, even if it was in bondage. In life and ministry, we are going to see and experience a lot of things that may discourage us from continually opening up our mouths so that He may fill it, but that is all a part of the process. Let our voices not be consumed by trials, rather let it be consumed with praises that are continually in our mouths (Psalm 34:1).

In the beginning, "God said." This is how we should start our day; let that be the fuel to your voice/vessel being filled, leading you to the land of milk and honey. In the beginning, God made me in His image and likeness. In the beginning of my life God showed me His love through my parents' love. In the beginning He showed me life through art, and it filled me with creativity. In the beginning, He made me an overcomer because He won it all. Declare whatever God told you at the beginning of your ministry, your childhood, your marriage, your business, or your vision, you name it. *Remember it and speak it out loud.* I once heard years ago that whenever you speak out loud, the thought in your mind has to align. For instance, if you say, "God loves me" out loud, it will be hard for any contrary thought to stand. Go ahead, try it. Let this be put into practice when you think that you are ill-equipped to write out that business plan that God said. Say to that mountain, "Nothing is impossible to those who believe in God. So, God, I ask you for help to write this business plan and I thank You for giving me resources and the strength to stay focused to finish this race." Take your faith *in action* (James 2:14). That's what God has been showing us since the beginning. I have spoken a lot about the importance of saying what God said and the authority in doing so, but what does God's voice *do*? We are called to remember His word, to speak His Word, but why?" …for our God is a consuming fire" (Hebrews 12:29).

The power of God's voice destroys, builds, heals, consumes, proves, and does what it was sent to do with all authority, in Heaven, Hell, and on Earth. Period. God is not like man that He should lie (Numbers 23:19). I believe that the familiar scripture, "And God said, 'Let there be light,' and there was light" (Genesis 1:3) is taken way too lightly.

I want to go over Genesis 1:1-4 slowly so we can get a clear picture detailing the impact of God's voice. The very beginning of The Bible starts by explaining what is happening in *"The beginning"*. You would think that was obvious, no? But then it reads *"God created"*. There is no timestamp, but more importantly, paints a picture of what this beginning looks like and is necessary to record. What does He create first? He created the Heavens and the Earth, something so vast and grand, yet no one has ever been able to duplicate it. Verse four continues by telling us that *"the earth was formless and empty"* - Which presents this question: This thing that God created had to be filled? It continues, *"Darkness was over the surface of the deep."* Wait, there's something *deep* but *empty*, and darkness was over the surface? So, something had to be underneath the surface, right? The last part of the verse tells us, *"And the Spirit of God was hovering over the waters."* But it just told me it was empty. (Hang in there with me, I'm taking you somewhere.) Verse five says *And God said, 'Let there be light,' and there was light.*

It is clear that in three short sentences, God did *a lot*, but He created and *then* spoke. And what He created far exceeds our understanding of what empty is. Verse four then said, "God called…" OK we know that God created, said, and called, all back-to-back. I want you to hear the very clear and strategic way God creates and brings things to life. What He sees as empty means there is no life there. If you notice, God was direct about everything and was focused. As the Great I

Am, if He thought it, said it and called it, it *would* be and come into existence. That very same *let there be light* in the beginning, is still at work today and is waiting for you to command light into every dark and empty place on this earth–in your life, your sister's life, into your womb, into your business, into your book, into your children and husband, and all of those we are to stand in the gap for and minister to.

As we remember that God is a consuming fire, let us know that it is because He is the One who is Holy (pure and perfect), there is none other like Him. His fire will speak for Him instead of letting Moses be consumed by His very presence. His very word spoke for Shadrach, Meshach and Abednego by sending an angel in the fire that was supposed to consume them. It's in the One who has eyes like Fire, the only One who can open the scroll and break the seal and sit on the throne that knows how to help you in times of trial and victory. We know that fire can essentially destroy or purify a thing or bring light and warmth. The presence and voice of the Lord is often referenced as fire in the Bible. So, if there is a fire in your life, ask the Lord who sent it and how shall this test purify you as His precious vessel in this season. Your perspective of adversity will change and remind you that I cannot be a warrior for the Lord without being violent. Just look at how flames of fire move violently!

I pray that everything you speak, or touch turns gold and that the mighty roar and fire of the Lord consume everything that is not like Him. I declare that you remember that you are His precious vessel and will not be moved as you abide in His presence. Let His love move you to the place He sent you,

Let His love cast out all fear. May you go to the dry land and say "let there be life!" and it springs up like rivers of living water!

We need you and God loves you. It's time for you to get your (*His*) voice back, now roar!

A Place of Divine Reflection

A Place of Divine Reflection

Constance Bridges

Connie Bridges is an ordained Minister and a natural-born leader who has faithfully served in many areas of ministry. She was reared in Raleigh, North Carolina, and educated in the Wake County Public School System. She went on to earn an Associate Degree in Business Administration. After twenty-two years of dedicated service, she retired from the State of North Carolina, Department of Health and Human Services. Connie accepted Christ as a young adult. Her grandmother, Mary Elizabeth White Mitchener, instilled in her biblical principles, Christian values, and the importance of living a lifestyle of holiness. This foundation prepared her to flourish spiritually and build a personal relationship with God.

For more than forty years, Connie has been a faithful member of Deliverance Cathedral of Love Church, where she serves as a pillar of strength and commitment to the ministry under the leadership of Bishop Nesbitt. From the words of Bishop Nesbitt, *"Minister Connie is a true pillar in the ministry. She lives by the Scripture: 'Whatever your hand finds to do, do it with all your might'* **(Ecclesiastes 9:10)**. Answering the call to ministry, Connie preached her initial sermon on March 5, 2023. Her favorite Scripture is **1 Corinthians 2:9**, which affirms her unwavering faith in God's promises. She currently resides in Knightdale, North Carolina.

Contact Evangelist Connie:

Email: c93778@bellsouth.net

Facebook: https://www.facebook.com/LadyConstance

"Flawed With Purpose"

Looking for Validation in All the Wrong Places

by Evangelist Connie Bridges

Growing up as an only child in a rural town of South Carolina called Wahalla, where it seemed that the whole town was nothing but red clay dirt, I always felt that I was different, not in a bad kind of way but that it was more out there in life, and I had to go get it. I had other first cousins that I was around because we all stayed in one big house together with our grandparents. We slept together, played together, went to school together and went to church together. We even had a little family singing group and oftentimes we played church together in the big front room of my grandparents' house. As a little girl I seemed to always want approval from my mother. It wasn't until I was at the age of forty that I ever heard the works from my mother's lips that she was proud of me. Even after then I guess I had waited so long to hear, it really didn't faze me any longer. By then I had been married for twenty-one years, had two sons and two grandchildren; I guess that it was more of a relief for her to tell me rather than me really feeling the need for her validation after all this time. Even though I had confidence in myself at that point there seemed to still be that need there when God was beckoning me to preach his word.

A critical point in life is to remember who you are, be true to yourself and to God as he has the last say so regarding your life not man! It is so easy to get caught up in what you think may be the right thing to do when it really is not. Before you know if you are fully engaged, years have passed, and you seem to be so caught up with it seems like everything is okay and the way that it should be. We all have purpose in this life; God has each of us here on this earth to fulfill a purpose. It is Him that has made us and not ourselves. He puts in us everything that we need, we just have to realize it and know how to cultivate what's on the inside, be confident of what we have and move forward. Most of the time it is us holding us back. Yes, there are stumbling blocks placed in our way, which may be people, places or things. Life circumstances happen to all of us, as they say, "Life be Lifeing" but God is still God and He is still on the throne.

I had been a part of the church for many years, attending service, working faithfully in every capacity that had been assigned to me and few that had not been assigned but because no one else wanted to do it, I stepped up to the plate. I had heard the preaching of the word every Sunday morning, Sunday night, Wednesday and Friday night; every revival and special service that we had I was there right there for it all, yet there was still something missing. It was not until the onset of COVID 19 hit the United States of America and I was at home and able to get still and look at everything that I had gone through over the fifty something years of my life that I began to evaluate some things. I was given some advice to take a deeper look at my relationship with the Lord. I knew that I was saved, sanctified and filled with the holy ghost but did I really have a relationship with God like I thought I had. I began to study the word of God more and of course with nowhere to go I certainly had more time to pray and seek the Lord. As my time with the Lord grew more my relationship with Him changed, it was strengthened, and God began to speak to me about myself. At that time when God spoke to me about myself, I had to repent and ask God for forgiveness because I was worshipping the creature more than the creator. I began to listen more attentively as he provided instructions to me, and it became more profound what I needed to do. Sometimes it was a little bit scary, you know when you are not used to God speaking to you and now it's like you are having constant conversations with Him and so many things are being brought to light in your life, it is really scary.

I realized in my life at the age of fifty-two, I was seeking approval from man, not even realizing that God had already given me His stamp of approval and that was all that I needed. After working in the church for many years, faithfully and tirelessly giving of myself, my time and my money to make things work out right in lots of situations, as I would tell myself, I had come to a place in my life that I got what some would say was a "wake up call". My grandmother brought me up in the church and taught me the fear of the Lord. She also instilled great morals and godly principles in me from the age of nine years old until I was fifty-two, and she transitioned from earth to glory at the age of 100 years of age on her birthday, January 21, 2020. As she was in her final days of life, she whispered some golden nuggets to all her close family including me. She told me as she had told me so many times before,

"Connie, I know that you love your Pastor and your church, but all your work is not in the church. God has a work for you to do."

I agreeingly nodded my head and said, "yes ma'am grandma, I hear you," having no idea at that time that in a few years that I would be preaching. I've always been a person to talk to other women and encourage them, sharing with them things that I had gone through in my life and telling them that God would keep them and that they could be somebody in life regardless of what their past was like. Not knowing that later in my life that God would have me to minister to women and begin to host my own conference, but it's happening.

THE REVELATION

I began to realize that after many years of laboring with and beside someone that as much as I was looking for their validation and approval of me that I was never going to receive it. It just was not their nature to do so. A "thank you" or "I appreciate you" was the extent of what I got. As God began to open my eyes regarding things, I felt hurt, embarrassed, then angry. How is it that I have labored with you for so many years, yet you don't see the gifts in my life. Embarrassed that others in the church and outside of the church would speak a word of encouragement to me but I would just laugh and say thank you. Thinking to myself, the one person that I was expecting to speak into my life and give encouragement has not said anything to me about what they see in me. Angry at myself for allowing this to happen, yet for so many years, I could not see what others saw in me, or maybe it was not time for me to see it. Ecclesiastes 3 tells us that there is a time for everything, a season for every activity under heaven. I know that my time is not God's time, there is a set time for all things, and a season. Thank God for being a sovereign God and a merciful God that he gave me a second chance, He redeemed the time for ME. It is funny how things come full circle in your life and you don't realize it until it is actually happening. It's all in God's plan for your life, and it is Him that is in full control and not us.

GET UP FROM THERE

When I finally got myself together and began to seek the Lord for my purpose in life, as I laid in my bed one night God spoke to me in a very loud and distant voice that I knew without a doubt that it was God and I had heard what He said. He said" I validated you" and that was enough for me. Philippians 1:6 came to my mind,

"Being confident of this, that he who began a good work in you will carry it on to completion until the day of Jesus Christ."

A young woman in my church wrote an inspirational prayer journal some years ago and she put it like this, "When you stop depending on other people to validate you and believe that God already has validated you, then you can live life to the fullest", and she could have not said it any better than that.

As God began to speak to me during my time of prayer and reading His word, I began to get a better revelation of what God wanted me to do, now I just had to learn how to put it into motion. I had to seek assistance outside of my church because what I needed was not there. Don't misunderstand me, the anointing of God was there, the gifts of prophecy and certainly the manifestation of miracles, signs and wonders were there but so much was missing. I later began to understand that sometimes when you are taught one way that is what you understand and it seems to be working for you because that is all you know, that you become complacent with that which you know and have and you do not want to change, even it is for the better. When you know to do better, you should do better. Once I decided that it was truly up to me to do what I needed to do to go forward, I got myself together and got a little bold and went for it. I thank God for all that I went through in my life, it made me appreciate God the more and truly understand his grace towards me. Without God I would be nothing, we say that as a cliché, but I can say with and mean it with my whole heart. It is because of God that I can lift my hands and worship him in spirit and in truth. It is because of Him that I am who I am. God kept me even when I didn't know that I needed to be kept.

Being raised by a single mother who received public assistance with food, utilities and help from other family members; having a child at the age of 15; leaving home at the age of 16 with the child; worked a part time job, went to school and graduated with my class. I could have been a statistic but I was determined to make something out of my life, everyday was not a good day but with the help of a loving and faithful God, a praying grandmother and some wonderful family, friends and people of God that he placed in my life along the way, and some are still in my life today, I MADE IT!!! Jeremiah 29:11 states,

> "For I know the plans I have for you," declares the Lord" plans to prosper you and to harm you, plans to give you hope and a future.'"

TO WHOM MUCH IS GIVEN….

When God has called you to a purpose in life, He justifies you and then He glorifies you and that is all you need. You do not need approval from anyone else but God. Just to clarify things now, of course if you are in a church with a Pastor, by all means respect your leader and meet with them to let them know that God has placed a call upon your life but know that it is God who has called you and God is expecting you to do what He says to do.

God chose me. I did not choose myself; He called me unto Him and gave me right standing with him. 1 Peter 5:10 states,

> "... after you have suffered a while, the God of all grace, who calls you to His eternal glory in Christ will Himself perfect, confirm, strengthen and establish you."

In 2004 God spoke 1 Peter 1:10 to me one morning, and at that time I did not understand what the scripture meant or what it would mean to me later in life,

> "Wherefore the rather brethren, give diligence to make your calling and election sure, for if ye do these things, ye shall never fail; for so an entrance shall be ministered

unto you abundantly into the everlasting kingdom of our lord and Savior Jesus Christ."

MAKING THE CHOICE

Whatever you choose to do in this life do it with your whole heart. You don't owe anyone an explanation for how you choose to live your life. Set boundaries for yourself, it took me a long time to grasp this concept. Someone once told me that there is an anointing in saying "NO". It will be a great refreshing to you in the long run, you will see.

Know that everyone will not understand the work that God has called you to do, and it is okay. Someone wrote a Facebook post that said "When God called you it was not a conference call" it was just you and God on the line. First Peter the second chapter and verse 9 in the message bible says "But you are the ones chosen by God, chosen for the high calling of priestly work, chosen to be a holy people, God's instruments to do his work and speak out for him, to tell others of the night-and-day difference he made for you— from nothing to something, from rejected to accepted.

Go forth in your calling that God has called you to, He has already validated you, He trusts you and you are fully equipped with everything that you need!

It's already in YOU!!

A Place of Divine Reflection

A Place of Divine Reflection

Natalie A. Scott

Elder Natalie A. Scott is a dynamic executive coach, motivational speaker, and prophetic change agent committed to empowering individuals and organizations to thrive spiritually and professionally. A devoted wife, mother, worshipper, and prophetic intercessor, Natalie lives by the principle that without God, she is nothing. Pursuing the call of God on her life since 2015, Natalie has faithfully served under the leadership of Bishop Dr. Michael A. Baston and Pastor Dr. Tasha S. Baston and now continues her spiritual journey under Apostles Dr. Dexter and Gennette Howard in Charlotte, NC. Her heart for prayer and prophetic insight have made her a trusted voice for transformation and restoration. In 2017, Natalie founded *Laughing Sarah*, a ministry birthed from her testimony of overcoming infertility. Through it, she empowers others to break cycles of barrenness, emotionally, spiritually, and physically, and walk into wholeness and purpose.

She has hosted the annual transformative encounter entitled the Birthing Room. As the founder and CEO of Called to B.E., Becoming Excellence, she equips emerging leaders and executives through coaching, mentorship, and strategic development. Through her many accomplishments and academia, inclusive of her B.A., M.A., and Doctorate degrees, Natalie combines deep spiritual wisdom with psychological and business expertise. She is the proud wife of Minister Joseph R. L. Scott and mother to their miracle daughter, Naiyah.

Contact Prophetess Natalie:

Email: iamlaughingsarah@gmail.com

Facebook: https://www.facebook.com/iamlaughingsarah

Instagram: www.instagram.com/iamlaughingsarah

Website: www.calledtobe.org

From Barren to Birthing

by Prophetess Natalie Scott

I never thought I would become a preacher, not based on a lifestyle but simply because I didn't see myself as worthy enough. Going to the church house was something I always liked doing. It became a part of my identity. I remember begging my mother to take me to Sunday school or dropping me off at my Godmother's church, a small distance from my house. It was not my local assembly, but it was a place in which I felt community. I loved dressing up, seeing people pray, and experiencing the warm embrace from my Godmother or receiving a piece of candy from a friendly, seasoned saint. I would beg my mother to take me to church until I asked her, "why are you not going, mommy?" I remember her looking at me, saying you know what, baby, today is the day I go. I need to develop my relationship with God.

She got up, got dressed, went to church, and at the end of service she joined the church. Then, my aunt and cousins, who had recently migrated to this country, got up, dressed, went to church, and joined. Then, the following week, with tears streaming down my face, I joined the church and decided to give my life to God. By all standards, the church I was raised in was nice-looking; in all accounts, that seemed like a growing church, yet it was not originally a place where they spoke in tongues or developed gifts. They did not initially believe in women in ministry; in all aspects of what can be seen from the outside, the question could be, why did you stay? I stayed because I heard the voice of the Lord. I could never articulate what I saw in people behind the clothes and the smiles. I never knew that it was the giftings and the anointing in my life.

I was at the crossroads of familiarity and destiny from an eight-year-old to an early twenty-year-old. I craved something more, I desired something more, I cried for something more, and God heard my heart. One day, God said to me so loudly and clearly,

> **"Don't leave. I have something more for you."**

That still, small voice who journeyed with me during difficult points of my life was the still, small voice who was allowing me to wait on my midwife. The Holy Spirit spoke to me, and I obeyed; I would not abort my destiny, no matter how uncertain I felt. So, on a cold spring day, a beautiful young woman and her new husband came to our church while I was dealing with debilitating depression. I remember not wanting to be bothered, nor did I want anyone to bother me. So, I found myself in the back of the church crying at the rocks, and that's when the Lord sent a woman of God to see past my current situation. Although I wiped my tears and tried to muster enough strength to seem as if I was all right, I was far from it. This young woman came up to me and looked me deep in my eyes, and she said,

> **"I see so much beauty behind those tears. Let me help you."**

With reluctance and simply hearing the voice of God speak to me, I could trust her. So, I did. I trusted a woman I barely knew, who became my first lady and spiritual mother.

I remember seeing changes happen before this moment, and I did not think much of it because I was blinded by what I felt. Before my late Bishop passed away, he ordained a woman into ministry who was faithful to the church for many years and received her doctorate in theology. The first woman in which my late Bishop ordained was tired of being overlooked and not acknowledged for her faithfulness. With holy boldness, she spoke up for herself and paved the way for other women to be ordained into the ministry. A year later, he ordained and installed my new senior pastor and his wife as Elders in the Lord's church. This was the start of a new era and chapter in my life. I finally got to experience what it was like to be awakened, develop who I am, and become in God.

I became this young couple's first spiritual daughter. I didn't know what it meant to be a spiritual daughter, yet there were times when they would call me to the church for prayer in the middle of the night. I would lie at the altar while they prayed for me, and I would not get up until I felt a release. They allowed me to see them at the start of their ministry, and I was observant, watchful, and prayerful. My now spiritual father was excelling in his career in higher education, and his wife was taking New York by storm. As humble as they were, this young couple is still reachable and touchable. The more I stayed close, the more I started feeling the chains break off me.

I became free through years of training, personal counseling, and much prayer. Once I became free, I felt an insatiable hunger to serve God. My leaders helped develop my gifting as an intercessor and servant. During those years in which I followed them to other churches and prayed for them, I didn't realize they were training me to be an armor bearer and a servant of the living God. I remember my natural mother thanking them for taking time from their schedules to help me. As I started praying and seeking God's face, I started seeing young women drawn to me. I remember the more I prayed, the more I felt God's presence. The more I prayed, the more I wanted to dance, and the more I prayed, the more I wanted to assist any other young person with low self-worth. I could sense, smell, and recognize it, the look of someone going through deep trials and tribulations. After a while, my spiritual parents started calling me a "seer" and introduced me to other ministry gifts, which they trained and imparted. I was fortunate enough to have leaders who taught me and introduced me to others who could train me in different parts of myself.

Two years into their ministry of being senior pastors, my spiritual father asked to speak with me, and he began to tell me about the story of Phoebe. He gave me the breakdown of other women in the Bible and told me,

"Natalie, it's time for you to really answer the call to ministry."

I was a minister. No way, I was a girl who just got delivered from depression and would party on Saturday and come to church on Sunday. He's undoubtedly not talking about me, but they saw something in me more than I saw in myself. I started to lead the youth ministry and dance ministry and began to preach at youth services around New York City.

Several years later, I met my husband at a dinner party with a couple of our mutual friends, who attended an event where I was the guest preacher. That conversation intrigued him, and he asked me a bold question while pointing at me:

You are?

The table got silent, waiting for me to answer his question, and I told him, "I'm Evangelist Natalie, and you are?" He said, "Well, evangelist, how does your church feel about Christian hip-hop artists?" I told him we were good with that, and I would love to exchange information for Kingdom purposes. At the time, I was intrigued, yet I just allowed him to put his information on my phone. We spoke the next day for eight hours, and I knew I felt safe and familiar. I never knew that this, by chance, meeting would be the next leg of my ministry. I would now enter the ministry of marriage. I realized I could feel safe, heard, loved, and supported. This was a different type of love that I never felt before romantically. I could be my most authentic self in every aspect of my being. Two years after our marriage, I became a licensed minister, and things started taking off. But nothing would prepare me for that one aspect of my heart I desired as a little girl: to be a mother.

My husband and I did not want to have children right away. We wanted to enjoy each other and the new life we were building. We were new homeowners. He was finishing up his degree. I was at the height of my career, but then I started to have an insatiable desire to be a mother. So, I got off birth control, and I thought the journey to motherhood would be easy, boy. Was I wrong? Once, I did not get pregnant or have my period for almost a year. After trying, my OB/GYN suggested that I see a reproductive endocrinologist. A reproductive endocrinologist, oh, this person was going to check out my hormones, yet I didn't realize my doctor was sending me to a fertility specialist. When I went to fill out the paperwork, the receptionist asked me if I was coming because of infertility.

Facing the fact of being labeled infertile hit me like a ton of bricks. A room with other women who were dealing with barrenness, but I just could not come to terms with the fact that I was going to go through this. Intrusive thoughts began to flood my mind; I started thinking about some of the sins from my past and saying that this diagnosis was due to my early years of promiscuity.

Who was the person who prayed for others, and they got pregnant?

There was no way I was being labeled as "infertile." This part of my life was no longer facing spiritual infertility but natural infertility. I felt broken, hurt, and confused. My mother had four children quickly. Indeed, this was not happening to me. But it was I was getting my blood drawn every other day and being poked and prodded and tested and tried, all while praying for others. People were receiving their breakthrough, their healing, and their deliverance, but I was in pain. Yet, after about three months of trying to figure out why I could not conceive, I was diagnosed with a pituitary brain tumor and PCOS. In the months that followed, I went through several surgeries, shots, pills, and painful procedures to heal the scarring on my uterus, but it could not heal the scarring on my heart. I kept my fertility journey a secret. Only my immediate family and spiritual parents knew that I was going through this. On New Year's Day 2017, I sat at a party where a couple I prayed for several months ago announced that they were expecting their first child.

The party's host turned around to me and said,

> **Natalie, what's wrong with you? Why are you not having a baby?**

One of my friends who knew my story quickly whisked me away to the back because I felt as if I would fall on the floor and cry. The host had no clue that asking me that excruciating and insensitive question triggered an unresolved issue. I ran into the host's bathroom and sobbed. My cries began to be so loud, so painful, so raw—the entire party per my cries. The host had no idea that she hurt me to my core; her husband also apologized to my husband. Once I came out of the bathroom, I mustered enough strength to educate her and the room about not asking couples when they would have a child. That night became a night of healing, compassion, and acceptance.

A couple of months later, more women randomly entered my inbox asking me to pray for them about having a baby. I will take their numbers down, then call them and pray for them, and they will receive divine healing through our Lord and Savior, Jesus Christ. In the spring of 2017, the Lord spoke to me and said,

"Natalie, I want you to create a ministry and safe space that will assist men and women dealing with natural and spiritual infertility."

When the Lord spoke to me about making this space, I had no idea how I would give birth to this ministry in what seemed like a barren place. I asked my husband for his thoughts, and he said, "if God told you to do it, I would support you." We brainstormed ideas regarding the name of this ministry, and we came up with the name Laughing Sarah. Laughing Sarah was named as a reminder that Sarah received her restoration once she had Isaac. Sarah no longer laughed in disbelief at the possibility of having a child, but she laughed because she received what she was promised. So, Laughing Sarah was launched on the 9th month and 2nd day of 2017. This date was significant because it happened in the month of birthing, and it was my birthday. I launched an elegant gala to signify the beauty of a painful topic. People came to the launch in their finest attire. There was such excitement and expectancy once I launched this ministry.

As I began to post and pray, I received inquiries from other women to assist them in starting their own organization regarding infertility awareness. I was now deep into my fertility treatments, yet I still got online and prayed. A couple of months into the journey of Laughing Sarah, I had a miscarriage. I did not realize that one of the fertility treatments worked. The doctor said it would take almost a miracle for me to get pregnant. I did not know what was going on with me. When I went to the clinic, they gave me hefty painkillers and told me that they would take one month off for me to rest. I still served and still was faithful to the work of the Lord. In November of 2017, while I was taking my lunch break, I walked down a hill and heard the Lord say that **"her name shall be Annalise."** The name Annalise means graced by God's favor.

The following month, December of 2017, my spiritual father and mother announced that I was becoming an Elder at the Lord's church. At my ordination, my spiritual mother declared that I was in my exodus season. As she gave me a prophetic declaration, I felt my womb pop. In the last two days of December, I made a declaration that this would be the last year that I dealt with infertility. I had my previous IUI and went to New Year's Eve service, not knowing that I had conceived our miracle child. In January of 2018, I had to minister at a women's retreat and realized I was pregnant. God worked a miracle because he did not forget about my husband and me. When I returned home from the retreat and went to do my blood tests, I received the best news in the world: I was going to be a mother, and my husband would be a father. We held each other and cried and thanked God for remembering us. I was so excited and afraid to share the news with anyone. Yet one of the first calls I was going to make was to my oldest brother, who was to wish him a happy birthday and let him know that his little sister would be a mom. He never received my birthday wishes or answered my phone call; my brother died in his sleep two days after his 50th birthday. The first funeral I conducted as a newly ordained clergy was for my brother. I was carrying God's prophesied promise, all while dealing with immense grief. After returning from bereavement leave, I was notified that my position was being eliminated due to budgetary issues. The pain that I felt was unbearable, but I had to stay positive because I was carrying my prophesied gift.

While pregnant, I applied for several jobs but to no avail, yet I still did the work of the Lord and did not back down from Laughing Sarah. My family and I had our gender reveal in the spring of 2017, in which I found out I was having a little girl. Fast forward, our prophesied gift was born one year after the launch of Laughing Sarah. Our graced favor was born in the month of birthing. I knew this was a part of God's plan. Add a reminder that giving birth in a barren place was so much more than a natural birth; it was also spiritual. A couple of years later, I got back on my feet and received a well-paying position, and my ministry was doing well. Our daughter was a natural reminder of what God can do, and now it was time to give birth to a spiritual movement.

In September of 2022, the birthing room experience was developed as a place for men and women to give birth to their gifts, talents, and anointing. Before I launched the birthing room experience, the Lord spoke to me and said to me,

> **"Natalie, I gave you your natural baby. It's time to give birth to a movement much larger than yourself."**

This was the first time I would put on a conference of this magnitude under the laughing Sarah brand. It was not my program but God's program. Within three days in the presence of the Lord, great deliverance, healing and revelation was done. Many of the participants gave birth to their ministry books and workshops and were free from past trauma. After all the years of not feeling capable enough, smart enough, or simply good enough, I realized I was no longer in a barren place but full of fruit. I made a promise to God that whatever he told me to do, I would do. Wherever he told me to go, I would obey the Lord even if I felt uncertain. During the birthing room experience, my spiritual mother said my name was changing again. It was no longer going to be Elder but now Prophetess. I was unbelievably shocked at that moment and humbled by being a mouthpiece of God. I promised God that I would be a midwife to assist anyone who felt barren, broken, and as if they were not in God's timing. It was my job to help shake the status quo. In July of 2023, I officially walked into the office of the prophet. The next day, I moved from a place of familiarity into a place where I did not have my immediate family and the comfort of my home church. This move caused me to depend more on God, cling closer to my husband, and raise our child without outside influences. Now, I'm a full-time minister, wife, mother, doctoral student, and entrepreneur, but mostly, I'm a child of the king.

When I moved from New York to North Carolina, God reminded me That everything would not be easy, but I needed to trust God wholeheartedly. I no longer feel as if I'm in a barren place, but I'm in a place where I can give birth to purpose. Since moving to North Carolina, I have been able to minister to countries where speaking the name of Jesus can get them killed. I have also started training other women meant to be spiritual midwives. I have weekly intercessory calls and training regarding the purpose of prayer. I have also begun to appreciate the beauty of not having everything together. Being a midwife, you never know what may happen during birth, but one thing is sure: my heart is to help those who give birth to promise. My ministry has always been centered around prayer, and it is my life's experience that has birthed the sound of worship and deliverance.

From barren to birthing, was a notion that my experiences made me feel as I was not thriving. I or you the reader was never meant to stay in a place of pain; the pain was designed to agitate action to purpose. My husband and I are even closer through our experiences and convinced that God's hand is surely at work. Moving to North Carolina has allowed him and my daughter to develop a relationship on his paternal side. Yet these experiences of my life have always been about service and action. I'm allowing God to continue to mold me and make me who he has desired me to be. Feeling barren is only temporary because God fills me up and overflows blessings in every part of my life. Has it been easy being a woman in ministry no, but it is one of the most fulfilling aspects of my life to assist someone giving birth to a movement that is much greater than they could have ever imagined.

I'm more than just a woman in ministry; I am standing on God's promises.

A Place of Divine Reflection

A Place of Divine Reflection

Priscilla D. Williams

Dr. Priscilla D. Williams is a prophetic voice in the Kingdom of God, serving as a teacher and preacher of the Gospel for more than twenty-six years. Her spiritual growth has been shaped through years of teaching, training, and life experiences. With a background in Religious, Business, and Legal Studies, she was released into the Apostolic and Prophetic realm of ministry, operating as a prophetic psalmist who ushers in God's presence through worship.

In 2015, Dr. Priscilla birthed Priscilla D. Williams Ministries, through which she has launched several powerful assignments: *Early Morning Worship with Dr. P* (held every Sunday at 4 AM) *Building God's Kingdom* (a teaching platform), and *Destiny Diamond* (a mentorship program for women). She is also the owner of Elite Events and Consulting Firm. In 2023, she released her first book, *Daddy, Where Are You? (I Am Your Daughter)*, which shares her personal journey of faith and healing.

She is actively affiliated with Word World Harvest Fellowship, the Southern Jurisdiction Conference, and the International Police and Fire Chaplains Association.

Above all, Dr. Priscilla is a daughter of God, a true worshipper, and an anointed vessel who has sacrificed much to follow Christ. Her favorite scripture is Psalm 24:1: *"The earth is the LORD's, and everything in it, the world, and all who live in it."*

Contact Dr. Priscilla:

Email: drpdwministries40@gmail.com

Facebook: https://www.facebook.com/priscilla.d.williams.3

Instagram: https://www.instagram.com/priscillad

The Divine Sacrifice

By Dr. Priscilla D. Williams

Hello, my name is Priscilla Denise Williams - you can call me Priscilla.

I am a daughter, sister, auntie, and friend.

I am an Entrepreneur (Elite Events and Consulting Firm) and an Author (Daddy Where Are You, I Am Your Daughter).

I have worked in the corporate setting for over twenty-five years My lasting employment is at an Aerospace in my hometown of Wilson, NC. I am well educated in the Legal arena, (AAS degree in Paralegal) and the religious arena (degrees from AAS to Doctorate), and of course I am a minister of the Gospel - a leader, mentor, counselor, and much more in the body of Christ.

I have been in ministry for over twenty-six years. I started ministry in 1998, at the age of twenty-two. I come with many skills, talents, and experience under my belt. The reason you're here is to hear my story of how I walked into this wonderful life of ministry in God. I want you to understand the life of a Woman in Ministry was not an easy walk but a journey worth taking.

As a young adult female, I want you to understand the ups and downs, the good and bad, the hardships and the struggles I dealt with in my mind, my heart and my spirit, the spiritual warfare I walked through with family, friends and colleges, that would make me want to lay it all down and turn away, but it was the foundation I stood on that kept me grounded, flat footed, and stable in chaos and this was before accepting the call of God on my life. My relationship with God is pure and insightful and most of all priceless; you can't make me doubt the God I serve. He knows what to do to make me know His love is true and real. I would not turn away from Him because of His goodness towards me. He is such an amazing God.

There will be much transparency here as I choose to share my journey. You will understand why the title of my chapter is called "The Divine Sacrifice". You will understand that the life I live cost me many friendships, family relationships and personal sacrifices; I took all for the sake of Christ Jesus, my Lord and Savior.

I pray my journey will help you to understand more about why we as women do what we must do to survive in this male dominated society, that you will come to understand that the warfare you endure is preparing you for your next and that realize that you are a necessary piece to the Kingdom of God.

So come and walk with me as I tell you my story of "The Divine Sacrifice."

WELCOME!

Part 1: Divine Sacrifice Began

I lived a very sheltered lifestyle as a young girl. I never experiencing the active out in the world, such as drinking alcohol, smoking, hanging out in clubs and bars, and living a promiscuous life. I grew up with church living and for the most part, was homebound. I literally grew up in the Baptist Church. I would say this many times "I was partially birth in the church", because this was all I knew.

My journey began at the age of fifteen, growing up with an older sister Mazzie Ann and a baby brother, Quentin. I was the "knee baby" or what we call the middle child. My mother Dorothy and grandmother Mazzie raised us the best they could with the help of the Lord. My sister Mazzie Ann was born with Cerebral Palsy (CP).

[1]*Cerebral Palsy is a disability that disforms the body. Here is the definition: a group of conditions that affect movement and posture. It's caused by damage that occurs to the developing brain, most often before birth.*

As the middle child, I found myself lost in the middle of the siblings, my sister with CP, had my mother's attention 24/7 because of her condition. She was unable to do anything for herself, such as combing her hair, walking or talking. She was fully dependent on our mother. For my brother, he was a grandmom's baby, and wherever grandmom went, he was right there. For me I had to find my place in this circle sometimes.

My sister was having some physical issues going on in her body and needed surgery. This was the fall of September 1991. Entering the hospital for minor surgery became a

---

[1] (Mayo Clinic, 1998-2024 Mayo Foundation for Medical Education and Research (MFMER, online))

nightmare for me. On Friday, September 13, 1991, it became the worst day of my fifteen-year-old life. My sister and I shared our birthdays in the month of August. She was born on August 28, and I was born August 22; she had just turned 18 and I had turned 15. My sister was scheduled for surgery on Friday, September 13, my grandmother, brother and I were going up that afternoon to see her and mom.

Because my sister was disabled my mother had to always be with her. As the day ended, strange things were happening around me, which allowed me to know that things were not going well for my family. Not knowing I was walking in the prophetic, it was operating in me at a young age. That afternoon she passed away during surgery. I lost my best friend, my big sister. I think about her, and tear up because number one, this was the first death I've encountered this close to me and number two, I had to find out what to do next without my sister with me. I stood at the door of her room with a blank look on my face and a heart that was broken, I had no clue as to how to fix it.

From that point, I had to get some answer from somewhere as to what just happened, and why it happened and where to go next. I was empty, confused, unsure, and lost. Does anyone understand what I'm saying? Yea, this was a mighty blow for all of us.

I was lost in this gigantic world alone. Remember now, I grew up in the church, so you would think I knew what to do next. Nope, I went to church but my relationship with God wasn't there but after this encounter my whole being changed.

One night, while resting in bed, I went into a deep sleep, and I saw myself floating in orbit; nothing but darkness. I mean darkness all around me, I was lost in space, literally. I was looking around to the left and right, up and down, front and back but I had no clue as to why I was there, what it all meant and why I experiencing that moment? There was much fear inside of me, I was scared, okay, yea scared. Thoughts ran through my head- Was I dead? Was I between Heaven and Hell, or was it where you end up when you died? There were many things going through my head but the revelation I received from this experience was 1. There's a place beyond where I am now on the earth; 2. Out of the darkness you can create your own reality of life, be a creator.

Orbit meaning, (a.) is a path described by one body in its revolution about another (as by the earth about the sun or by an electron about an atomic nucleus); (b.) a circular path. (Meriam-Webster © 2024 Merriam-Webster, Incorporated)

1 In the beginning God created the heaven and the earth.

² And the earth was without form, and void; and darkness was upon the face of the deep. And the Spirit of God moved upon the face of the waters.

³ And God said, Let there be light: and there was light.

⁴ And God saw the light, that it was good: and God divided the light from the darkness.

⁵ And God called the light Day, and the darkness he called Night. And the evening and the morning were the first day.

Genesis 1:1-5

When God created the earth, it came out of nothingness, into something but it only came about by the words that came out of His mouth. God spoke life into "that" which never existed and now exists and functions. When you open your mouth and spoke the words, "Let there be and there was". When I got out of this dream, I sought the Lord for instruction and guidance.

Part 2: Then Divine Sacrifice in Tribulations

This experience brought me to the point of asking God who I was to Him. What do you want me to do while I'm on this earth? I kept asking God, every day and every night as I was looking for answers. You get to a point when asking the same question gets old and you want to give up and move on and I was at that point. Until one day I was reading the Old Testament scriptures of 1 Samuel 3:1-10.

¹ And the child Samuel ministered unto the Lord before Eli. And the word of the Lord was precious in those days; there was no open vision.

² And it came to pass at that time, when Eli was laid down in his place, and his eyes began to wax dim, that he could not see;

³ And ere the lamp of God went out in the temple of the Lord, where the ark of God was, and Samuel was laid down to sleep;

⁴ That the Lord called Samuel: and he answered, Here am I.

⁵ And he ran unto Eli, and said, Here am I; for thou calledst me. And he said, I called not; lie down again. And he went and lay down.

⁶ And the Lord called yet again, Samuel. And Samuel arose and went to Eli, and said, Here am I; for thou didst call me. And he answered, I called not, my son; lie down again.

⁷ Now Samuel did not yet know the Lord, neither was the word of the Lord yet revealed unto him.

⁸ And the Lord called Samuel again the third time. And he arose and went to Eli, and said, Here am I; for thou didst call me. And Eli perceived that the Lord had called the child.

⁹ Therefore Eli said unto Samuel, Go, lie down: and it shall be, if he call thee, that thou shalt say, Speak, Lord; for thy servant heareth. So Samuel went and lay down in his place.

¹⁰ And the Lord came, and stood, and called as at other times, Samuel, Samuel. Then Samuel answered, Speak; for thy servant heareth.

I read this scripture several times, then prayed to the Father and went to bed. I did this for serval months. During the process I receive instruction, dreams, visions, and guidance. I would begin to hear voices; mind you I was still young but growing in God and learning. Just like the disciples, I was unlearned but as I walked this journey I was learning as much as I could. It was during this time, around 1995-1997, I graduated high school and now entered college, to pursue my AAS in Paralegal at our local community college, with plans to graduate in 1997.

I began hearing a voice in my heart, but I could not understand what was being said clearly. I found myself in a quiet place of worshipping God and singing to Him. I would have a familiar prophet playing music during my down time with the Lord. I grew to love the Father so deeply that I could not go a day without spending time with Him. I didn't care where I was, I would listen to the worship music and have quite time with the Father. This became my lifeline when I would find myself in some dark place in my life. Even though I was growing spiritually and was also experiencing life here on earth. Now out of high school into college, I had bills to pay, and I needed a job, so, I did part time at a local dollar store and went to school on my schedule days, church on Wednesday bible study and Sunday services, and I was very active in the community as well. I was in a few organizations for women and civil group. I was a very active young lady. When I got to the place I could distinguish between God's soft voice and my mind talking to me. I was able to understand what God was speaking in my spirit.

One reason why I was so active was that I needed to fill the void I had, which my sister Mazzie Ann left. Still healing from my sister's death was not easy. There were days when I when fell into a spirit of depression, not knowing it was depression, but I would find myself crying to the point I cried myself to sleep. Yea, those moments are real in much of our lives.

1998 came, and I was in a place where people were speaking into my life about preaching the gospel and traveling with the gospel. One prophet spoke, "they saw me on great platforms"; so much word was given to me during this time of my life. My Bishop would talk to me about preparing to preach the Word of God, but I would say "naw" Bishop. I love teaching Bible study to the young people and working with the youth in the church. I worked in many departments within my church, but one night God wanted to talk, so I laid there talking to the Father most of the night.

The next big obstacle in my journey that had to face was denominational barriers within my household. There is a religion that does not believe women preaching the gospel or wearing pants in the church house or anywhere for that matter. You may know this denomination, if not walk with me on this journey. Theres nothing against leadership or the members, the structure and traditional mindset of the people way back the female gender from operating in their calling for God.

My grandfather was a leader in this body, they called their Pastor's "Moderator" for this. My grandfather passed away when in was around 2-3 years old, but my grandmother still operated in this same traditional mind set for year. Being a 1st Lady, she continued my granddaddy's legacy, which including the belief that women had no place in the pulpit preaching the Word.

The scripture they referred to, was the conversation Paul had with the women, to remand quite while male leadership was speaking, the scripture reads.

1 Corinthian 14:33-34

^{33b} As in all the churches of the saints, ^{34} the women should keep silent in the churches. For they are not permitted to speak, but should be in submission, as the Law also says. ^{35} And if they desire to learn anything, let them ask their own husbands at home; for it is improper for a woman to speak in church.

"It would be like allowing them to teach and to exercise authority—something that he clearly prohibits in 1 Timothy 2:12: *"I do not allow a woman to teach or exercise authority over a man, but to remain quiet.""*

(IX 9Marks, Must Women Be Silent in Churches? (1 Corinthians 14:34)

Yep, those scriptures. So, this was the short version of why Paul said what he said. Paul wasn't angry, upset or frustrated with the women, it was nothing like that. If you know protocol, you would know, when in service, your leadership conducts the service and flow in the spirit of God. During this time, in the service was in a prophetic flow of worship (1Corinthian 11:5), and the prayers and worship became overwhelming, Paul simply wanted the women to begin lowering voices so that the headship (Pastor/Lead) could operate in his prophetic flow. If you know the scripture, God doesn't operate in confusion, He was only speaking through leadership. In the early scripture Paul did not rebuke the women from speaking, he welcomed it and even instructed them on how to operate in it correctly. If you needed more understanding when you get home talk to your husband. There is much more to say on the matter but for another day.

So, this Christian body, took this scripture and many more out of context. While growing up, that was all I heard in my grandmother's conversation on the phone, "they were gossiping", when talking about women they knew in ministry and even some of the women in knew. Gossip is a piece I care nothing about because it hurts, harms and destroys other people in so many ways. I never cared for it. With that being said, I knew that this would be a "hard nut" to crack, and I was sacred to say anything to her.

Now, this part lets me know that God was in the midst of my calling. It's still 1998, I was a college graduate, I was working part time at a Law firm and still at the dollar store. During this time my grandmother got sick one day at home, she went to the doctor, and they found cancer in her body. The obstacle within the obstacle that we all had to face. During this time, I was my grandmother's driver. Chemo treatments, paying bills, grocery shopping etc. I learned a lot in that year from my grandmother. I also watched God transfer her during this time in her life. It took this to get my grandmother to a place of knowing, loving and accepting Christ in her life. No, I still have not said anything, but God was still speaking. It came to a point where grandmother got worse physically, that she would have to go to a facility in our capital city for assistance.

In spite of the battle, yes, I accepted the calling on my life, I spoke to my Bishop; with a big smile on his face, he scheduled the date and all in one setting, okay!

So now I need to talk to grandmom. I sat at her bedside and told her that God has called me into the ministry, and that I had accepted the call. My heart was pumping very hard at that moment, but low and behold my grandmother gave me her blessing. She understood by this time that no one could stop a move of God or be that stumbling block in anyone's life.

Though grandmom was a part of my warfare for years, I loved and respected her life. She was that strong, tough and nonstop individual. I am who I am because of my grandmother's firm hand and even firmer disciple level. I never wanted to be that way, but I needed it for the next part of my journey.

Part 3: The Divine Sacrifice of Myself

Sunday, November 22, 1998, I did my initial sermon, topic "Having Faith in GOD". I walked this whole sermon out for about seven years before preaching the message. I stood in a place that I had never been in before, it felt different but familiar to me. I created my story out of the dark place I was in seven years earlier. Family, friends, and co-workers were there to support me and celebrate with me but there were two people who were not physically there, that was my sister and my grandmother. I know my sister was my guardian angel and grandmom was praying for me where she was. I went forth to proclaim the Word of God, I went through the protocol of ministry and walked in my full calling at the age of twenty-two.

A year later Saturday, November 14, 1999, my Grandmother Mazzie Harris Coley left us. I was home with her alone. There was a song that was my favorite Primitive Baptist hymn, "There is Oil in My Vessel", I had that song sung at her service and my sister's service. Every now and then I would sing that song, remining me of the oil in my vessel is lit and burning bright and that should never let my flame go out for any reason. I should never allow anyone, or anything stop me from manifesting the works of God in the earth until he takes me home.

I'm now at a place where my life in Christ shifted to a realm that I have to use what I learned from my grandmother as a woman who doesn't play, meaning stand for who you are as a woman but most of all a WOMAN of GOD. Being the youngest female in our church ministry, I was given a position in the church that had me leading leaders and teaching leaders into their offices in ministry. I was appointed Youth Pastor of our church, number one we never had a young pastor ever and secondly director over the Ministerial staff of the church. I had serval other positions in the church where I lead the youth and adults, but I have to say I was equipped for it.

The Divine Sacrifice ~ My Personal Sacrifice to God

As a woman in ministry there are many sacrifices, we will take, some for our family and friends but there are sacrifices we must take for God. I was in a totally different season of my life which was obvious seven years later. Maturity in mind, in Spirit, in life had a lot more meaning to me as I walk as a spiritual leader to so many, a Pastor and Influencer. Walking in these offices brought great opportunities to fellowship with other leaders in my position. We collaborated with each other on ideas, events and possibilities to enhance the Body of Christ and our Youth.

The other side of being in this position as a young woman in ministry and SINGLE brought another type of warfare that always put me in protective mode. Please don't leave the church, change your mind about Christ, or judge everyone off my experiences. My experience when it comes to the male gender in the body of Christ was very shocking for a might long time. The few men I trusted around me were my Bishop and a few leaders in my church, maybe one or two outside the church, only because they were close to my Bishop, and I worked closely with him. When we lost our third Assistant Pastor to death I stood in that place to help Bishop and continue working my office as a Youth Pastor; I had a great staff, so they made it easy for me to do what I did.

I kept silent for a long time because of what I saw behind closed doors, open doors and glass doors. As a woman of God, I made a promise to God that I belonged to Him mind, body, soul and spirit and I was very serious about that piece in my life. My Promise Scripture Romans 12:1-2, has remand relevant in my life up to now.

The scripture reads:

[1] I beseech you therefore, brethren, by the mercies of God, that ye present your bodies a living sacrifice, holy, acceptable unto God, which is your reasonable service.

[2] And be not conformed to this world: but be ye transformed by the renewing of your mind, that ye may

prove what is that good, and acceptable, and perfect, will of God.

There was an encounter that I was very uncomfortable in with a clergyman, older than me, and with the issues I were already dealing with, with my male counter parts, I ask God to help me with this warfare. Romans 12:1-2 was a scripture that spoke to my heart from God. Even before ministry, this scripture I decreed over my life, that I keep body, this vessel for God only, "The Divine Sacrifice". For me it was very important God could use me fully, whole and purely. It was very important to me because it was important to Christ. I allowed no man to come and take what did not belong to them, only to the God Man, my Father has for me. So, for twenty-six years I've allowed no man to break My Promise to God. When I preach, I want to preach with clarity, power and wisdom straight from God himself. He has honored my request and still today we remain as one, working in the body of Christ saving, teaching and pouring out life to the dead and lost.

Growing up, I did not have my dad in the household with me, so there were many things I felt I missed out on as a little girl. I didn't have those father daughter talks; the conversation you should have on how to handle certain situation when it comes to the male species. I had many trust issues when it came to dealing with males in personal relationships and knowing how to embrace them in an open, friendly and sisterly/brotherly way.

This was a great struggle for me, for years. You can read my book

"Daddy Where Are You, I AM You Daughter, Vol 1"

(REZIPRINT, copyright 2023 by Priscilla Williams)

Ministry was my life, I breathed it, ate it, lived it, and died for it. I never wanted to fail my Father for any reason, but let me tell you, you're not perfect it, you're not invincible, you're not the only one who can do the job. Believe me there is someone else who can do the job you're doing now and even better than. Never place yourself above other because you will surely fall and hard you will go. I've seen so many leaders fall and never get back up; there were a few who got through the tough terrain and came back but not without scars and broken reputations.

As Woman of God, your reputation is valuable, if you even damage your reputation because of sexual sin, conspiracy in the church of any kind or one of my favorites, not married/single woman. You are now the Whole, slut, man stealer, ''tch, and so many more names, you know them. Let me give you some of the name I was called. Because I was single and at an age where you should be married with children, I was considered a lesbian, also called the devil, the one mentioned earlier and in some cases I think some people just didn't know what to say. I got this for co-labors of the Gospel male and female, Leadership and Family. That warfare hit me hard and yes, my reputation was tarnished but I did not operate in those areas for years.

Yes, I dated, only males of course. I probably dated six guys, was in three serious relationships and one engagement with one attempt now. Dating as a single Pastor, I've got all types of text messages, you think it, I got it - phone calls, emails, picture and a few stalkers, too. Yep, you heard me right, I had I believe it was two stalkers, one in ministry and the other wasn't.

That is why I don't do blind dates or set ups by friends or family. I'm very selective of who I allow around me. It's a part of living the life of a single Pastor. I've dated guys outside of the church, meaning not close to God but know Him and has much respect for Him. I found myself enjoying their company much more than the saved guy. The saved guy can be too churchy and wants to go to service after service after service leaving us with little time with each other. Yes, there are restrictions you must have while dating but that's the area you two will have to talk about privately. The unsaved guy knows how to spend his time wisely. We'll go out to eat, watch movies, dine and music. I'm a jazz lover so take me to a jazz diner or a jazz club, yep, I said it. I don't drink nor do I smoke, but there are some clean and fresh environment venture you can go to and enjoy with your man. At the end of the day the choice is yours to make, who do you really want to spend your time with and who would you think God chose for you? You may be surprised at His choice for you. A story for later.

Now, I am not a perfect person, and I have made some foolish decisions without God and with God, there are none I would go back for but rather I will be moving forward in. Repentance is a life saver, use it, it's for your good.

I know you have questions to ask, let me guess.

1. Are you ashamed of being a virgin at this age?

I have someone very close to me who says you need to get some to release the tension or stress I deal with occasionally. I will never miss what I never had.

I'm not ashamed to live this lifestyle. I'm not the only virgin in the world; there are a few of us. My job is to please God not man. For man has no heaven or hell to put in so I'm good.

2. Do you desire marriage?

Yes, I most definitely desire to be married to the husbandman God has for me. My vision and type of man has changed dramatically from 26 to now at 47, the list had shortened.

The scripture from Luke 15:31 says

"I am my Fathers daughter, I am always with Him, and all that He has is mine."

I belong to God; I am His daughter indeed. I have not been the best daughter, but He loved me despite all my flaws.

I define myself as a "Quite Storm". A storm will come with advance notice; you already know that it's headed your way. But there are some storms that you will never know are coming until it's sitting at your door. I'm that storm you'll never coming. Why? Because "I'm hidden in that secret place of the Most High." Only God will reveal me in his due season. You are a gift, treasure, and DIMOND, yes, look it up. You're very rare, precious, and priceless.

To my single "Ladies in Waiting" never step down to their level but stand on the Word of God. I hope you received some nuggets from my journey in ministry that will encourage you to continue to walk forward in you calling and destiny in Christ Jesus.

You are NECESSARY.

Seasoned with Salt ~Preserved for this Journey!

God Bless You All, Dr. Priscilla D. Williams

A Place of Divine Reflection

Rhonda Hatton

Rev. Dr. Rhonda Royal Hatton serves as the Senior Pastor of Celebration Ministries, Lutheran, a thriving ministry she planted in Durham, NC. She is the devoted wife of Bishop Dr. Ian Hatton and the proud mother of two beautiful young adult daughters. Dr. Hatton holds both a Master's and Doctoral degree in Christian Ministry and Theology.

She is the Establishmentarian and Presiding Bishop of Royal Priesthood Fellowship of Churches, International, where she provides spiritual covering and mentorship to church leaders. In addition, she is the Founder and President of Royal Theological Seminary at Durham and the Founder and Artistic Director of Royal Priesthood Performing Arts, Inc., an arts-based nonprofit producing stage plays, women's empowerment conferences, and arts training classes.

A gifted poet and spoken word artist, Dr. Hatton has authored two poetry books and taught creative writing in middle school. With a bachelor's degree in Theater Education, she also served many years as a Theater Instructor at both middle and high school levels.

An internationally traveled missionary and preacher, Dr. Hatton has spent more than thirty years coaching and counseling others toward spiritual growth, emotional healing, and breakthrough. A true servant leader, she believes all people were created for greatness.

Motto: *"You were born great! Live into it!"* – **Jeremiah 1:5**

Contact Dr. Rhonda Royal Hatton:

Email: hattonrhonda@gmail.com

Facebook: https://www.facebook.com/rhondaroyalhatton/

Instagram: www.instagram.com/rhondalaree

Destined to Walk in My Calling: Talitha Cumi! Girl Get Up!

By Rev. Dr. Rhonda Royal Hatton

"For my thoughts are not your thoughts, neither are your ways my ways, declares the Lord." Isaiah 55:8

God has a way of messing with our ideologies by often calling us to the unfamiliar. God will at times, call us to serve in a way that may be uncomfortable, which requires a level of Faith that stretches us. Sara was told that she would have a child way beyond her season of childbearing; she laughed at first, but indeed Isaac was born. How many times in our lives have we heard God's voice in our prayers, in our dreams, or through other people that challenged our Faith concerning ourselves? We said, "that surely is not the voice of God; for that is impossible for me to achieve. Mary, the mother of Jesus, was chosen by God to carry our Savior although she was still a virgin. Her fiancé suspected that she had been unfaithful. He chose to privately end the relationship with this chosen vessel. The Angel of the Lord had to personally speak to Joseph and let him know that indeed God had chosen her to birth and raise the Savior of the world. Has God spoken to someone and they shared with you what seemed impossible for them? Then, because of our own thoughts and self- restrictions, did we say that it was not God? Even though we denied what God was saying to them, we could not deny the power of how God is using them in their area of calling? Then, why should we be surprised that God still calls us to service in ways that we are not used to? Similarly, God called me, Rhonda, to serve in the most unexpected way.

After being a founding member of a church, and serving there for twenty-two years, I found myself transitioning into another Ministry. This was something I never expected to happen because I had been serving there all of my young adult life. I thought I would serve there my entire life. I was planted there and never thought I would be uprooted in any way. But God had a different plan.

After attending seminary, a Lutheran church hired me to be their Outreach Minister. I was ecstatic to have a full-time job in ministry; working with the community, people of faith and college students. All the while, I continued to serve faithfully in my former church as I worked as the Outreach Minister for the Lutheran Church. After three years working for the Lutheran Church, God began to change my assignment. By this time, I had been serving in my former church for 21 years. God was transitioning me into the Lutheran Church full time because of what God was calling me to do and who God was calling me to become. My former church family treated my transition as betrayal. I was hurt to the core because of my love for them. This was a time of great deliberation and pain for me. I knew what it meant. I knew I could not do what God was calling me to do and remain at my former church. I also knew, if I left to pursue what God was calling me to and who God was calling me to be, it would cause me to be ostracized. I would no longer be considered family. My time served there would be removed from the church history. I would be removed from the hearts of those with whom I had spent all of my young adult life doing grassroots ministry. Oh, this was hard; but I could not deny God's calling.

So, after much prayer, with tears in my eyes and a broken and contrite heart, I answered, "Yes". God then spoke to me. God reminded me of the walk that Jesus walked. God reminded me that it was the spiritual leaders of Jesus' faith community that could not and would not see that He was the Savior and that He came to set the captive free. God reminded me that the people of Jesus' faith community could not get past who He had been; the son of the carpenter,

Joseph. God reminded me of the Garden of Gethsemane where Jesus prayed the fervent prayer, asking God to let the cup pass. God reminded me that I had agreed to drink of the bitter cup. God reminded me that there must be a cross to experience the resurrection. I had heard many a preacher say, "There is a cost for this oil." This was not an easy thing for me to do. I loved the church where I had served for over 20 years. I loved my former pastor and first lady. We had literally grown up together in the Ministry, but I knew that love was not enough to keep me there. The threat of being excommunicated was not enough to make me deny the call. I had to obey the calling of God even if it meant that my name would be blotted out from the history books of that Ministry. At that point, the most important thing was that God would not blot my name out of the Book of Life. God spoke to me, reassured me and touched me, as Jesus did to Jairus's daughter and said, "Talitha Cumi", being translated "Girl! Get Up! I had to rise from my place of slumber and tears and move into my destiny.

And what a destiny God had for me! In my former church, for 20 years, I served as a Missionary, doing ministry and missions in my local community and in-house. The first stretch God did was to call me to Seminary. At the time, I thought the Seminary was only for people who preached and pastored churches. I know better now, but then I didn't understand why God was calling me to go to the Seminary, I didn't plan on "preaching" or "pastoring" anybody. God told me that the Seminary would be a door- opener for me; that graduating from Seminary would allow me to usher the Holy Spirit into places that were unfamiliar to God's supernatural presence. I said "Yes". I applied and was accepted. While attending Duke Divinity School, I had the awesome opportunity to travel abroad to Africa and Brazil, doing missionary work. Although my original plan was to do Christian Education, God began to stoke the fire within me to preach the word. While working as the Outreach Minister for the Lutheran church, I was flown all over the country to train in Mission Development. I became a Mission Developer, which is a church planter. The Lutheran Church affirmed the call upon my life as a preacher and teacher of the Gospel. They advanced my Seminary training by requiring me to take courses at three different Lutheran Seminaries. I was so excited because I loved to learn. Little did I know that the entire time, God was setting things up.

Several years ago, I was attending my sister- in- the-Lord's wedding and a Prophet spoke these words to me and my husband. He said, "God is putting you both on the fast track. Many will feel that you are moving up in the Ministry too quickly, but do not fret. For the Lord is just catching you up to where you should have been. Think it not strange that because you made a major move in Ministry through Faith, eyes haven't seen nor ears heard the great things that God has in store for you." We didn't know him. We had never met him before. We heard him, we rejoiced, but at that time, we had no idea what that really meant.

After seven years of serving as the Outreach Minister in that local Lutheran Church, the program ended and God pushed me out of the nest to begin a Lutheran Missions Church. I became the founder and the pastor of an assembly of people! It was challenging. It was both scary and exciting! It was an unique opportunity. That Outreach Ministry developed into a congregation. I now know that it was God working His plan.

During this time, the Lord allowed me to fulfill what he told me in the beginning; that I would be able to usher in God's supernatural Spirit in unlikely places. God has connected me with many spiritual leaders and congregations. I have been ordained as an Elder, Prophetess, Pastor, Apostle and soon to be consecrated as a Bishop in an interdenominational organization. I have had the wonderful opportunity to teach and preach the Gospel all over the country. I have many apostolic and natural gifts and God has allowed me the opportunity to use them in the Ministry. I am a writer, actress, playwright, poet and Spoken Word Artist. The Lord has made ways for me to do Drama Ministry and share my spoken word gifts in many arenas – secular and sacred – all in the name of the Lord. I have had the humbling experience of helping to prepare, ordain and consecrate men and women as Elders, Ministers, Missionaries, Deacons, Evangelists, and Pastors in the body of Christ, and in the near future Teachers and Apostles. Who would have thought this? Definitely not I. I was content being Missionary Hatton, winning souls to Christ, helping to stabilize those in the body through serving. Then our great God called me from my place of contentment and challenged me to go forward in the midst of voices that I trusted and loved, but voices that were now not in agreement with my transition.

This journey has not been for the faint of heart. There has been much warfare as I have moved in the calling of God. Remember, there is a cost for this oil! No cross, no crown! When you see me moving in the power of our Living God, know that there was sacrifice, know that there was heartbreak, know that there were some tears, but our wonderfully, merciful God honors my- "Yes!" Our King Jehovah has been my fortress and my strength. I have had to fight in the

Spirit, through prayer. The enemy has attacked my character, my sincerity, my motives, and my authenticity. But we are not ignorant of the devil's devices. We must remember that the adversary called our Savior Jesus – Beelzebub! I have learned to trust God through it all. It is difficult at times; I will not paint pictures of rainbows but know that God is always with us. I fully understand now that those with a prophetic call upon their lives will experience rejection, misunderstanding, jealousy and envy. Know that Jesus came to do the will of the Father but was the stone that the builders rejected. When we answer the call of the Father, we too will experience rejection and persecution. Jesus rose with all power in His hands, and we will too. I am stronger because of the calling, and more determined because of it. I have fully accepted this unique call upon my life, and I RISE to fulfill it.

Your Life Changing Moment Today

Be influenced by God's call for you to arise out of the places of familiarity and complacency to serve His purposes with great opportunity. Let God challenge you through the new things He wants to do in your life. Even if it causes you to lose some friends, some statuses, and some other important things, know that God's call is greater! God will replenish, replace and renew everything that is sacrificed in your life!

Reflection

I. Were there times you have judged others, only to later realize that God was deeply working in the one who you judged so critically?

II. Were there times when you felt God's leading and your spiritual support system became the camp that was judging you, criticizing you, or even mocking you?

III. In both of these questions, what are the lessons we are to learn about God and how God moves and works in our lives and the lives of others?

Know that God has designed a personal journey for each of us. At some point in time, we have probably been on both sides; either we were judging the other person, wondering- "What in the world is he thinking?" or we are the one being called to build an ark in the desert!

PRAYER

Lord, help me to recognize that you are a God who doesn't fit in my box or the boxes of others. You will surprise us and reveal yourself in ways we never expected. Help me to accept this and look for your wonderful, unique ways of revealing your love and power within me, through me, to me, and through those that may be the least expected. Oh, God allow me to stretch without breaking, and to bend without snapping. I am your servant Lord, allow me to allow you to be You, and not squeeze your people into my limited understanding. Help me not to operate in self-righteousness and arrogance when it comes to the things of You. I desire to be open to all that you are doing in this season with others and with me. I annihilate the spirit of fear that would attempt to paralyze me, causing me to miss what the Lord has in store for me. Increase my Faith and my courage in this hour, to trust you God, in all uncomfortable situations that are ordained by You. Lead me, oh God, guide me that I may rise into my destiny that you have set before me. In Jesus's name. Amen.

I accept that with God, I am **destined to walk in my calling!**

Sharon Cotton

Apostle Sharon Denise Cotton was born on September 8, 1964, in Greenville, Mississippi, and raised in Boston, Massachusetts. She answered the call to ministry in 2003 under the leadership of Rev. Dr. Conley Hughes, Jr. In 2020, after hearing the voice of God directing her to transition from Concord, she was ordained as Pastor under Apostle Angela Smith, Pastor of Unstoppable Kingdom Ministries. Pastor Sharon is the founder of Kingdom Intercessory Ministries (KIM), a powerful prayer ministry dedicated to reaching souls through intercession, prayer conferences, and street evangelism. In addition to ministry, she is also a successful entrepreneur, owning Accessory Boulevard, known for its beautiful fashion jewelry, and Blessed Aromas, recognized for its fragrant oils.

She holds a master's degree in biblical studies from Gordon-Conwell Theological Seminary and is a Certified Life and Spiritual Life Coach, receiving her certification through Heart Christian University. Pastor Sharon faithfully serves as the Lead Intercessor for Church Without Walls in the city of Boston. Affectionately known as *Pastor Shae*, she was consecrated in May 2025 as Apostle under the covering of Apostle Deborah Vails of Set Free Ministries.

Her motto is "Sometime You Have to Take Part in Your Own Rescue"

Contact Apostle Sharon Cotton:

Email: kimpwhob@yahoo.com

Facebook: Kingdom Intercessory Ministries

YES, IT HURT, BUT GOD!

By Apostle Sharon Cotton

THE NERVE OF THEM ALL! As I open this chapter, I do so very cautiously to be certain that I am not placing blame or aiming at anyone but all that I say does factor into the Woman of God that I am today. So therefore, I say thank you, Jesus, that the truth comes from you because people will have you second guessing who you are and everything you stand for if you listen to them.

I remember early not only in my call to ministry but even as a little girl, I was brought up in church but after Sunday, my immediate surroundings look nothing like church, not that things were hellish but there wasn't much talk about Jesus once church was over but then on Saturday once again, we had to get those clothes ready for service the next day. My mother made sure we knew about Jesus, but we didn't know Him on a personal level if you get my drift. Please don't get me wrong, she was and still is a beautiful person, treated people kindly and would give you the shirt off her back if she had to, but the things we needed to know about Jesus to build our own relationships with Him, we lacked. And as for myself, my children grew up in church as well, went every Sunday, even sang in the choir and attended Saturday children's church but I must say, I didn't drive home what they needed to escape the wolves of this society. MY FAULT BABIES. It wasn't until I was older, and my children grew older that the necessity of a relationship with Christ began to develop. IT'S NEVER TOO LATE TO PURSUE THE MASTER OF OUR FATE.

However, like most black families, church on Sunday, Christmas and most certainly Easter was the thing to do and there lies the problem. Doing it because every generation before you did it. I'm certain that our ancestors, grandparents and all those before us meant well. But it is never okay to do a thing because someone else did it, However, it did plant the seed that needing a relationship with God was and still is a huge need for us all.

I remember my eldest daughter and I were having a conversation because my grandson asked me if he could be baptized, and her response was "no." I asked her why and she replied that she felt like she was made to do it at the age of seven and not that it was her personal choice. I stated that he asked but she wants him to be a little older so that he is sure of what he is doing. Well handing your children over to Christ can never be a wrong decision but they should be certain of the choice they're making. The bible is clear in "Luke 14:28-29" about counting the cost before building to make sure you can complete your projects or even your process.

MY EARLY DEVELOPMENTAL STAGE IN MINISTRY

I was very eager as I would sit in the balcony of our church in my favorite section and when my pastor would call for prayer and he would say to let our voices resonate throughout those high ceilings. I was new to praying both silently and out loud, so once my mentor uncle taught me that all I had to do was start talking and the Holy Spirit would take over from there. Well needless to say, that's exactly what happened. But then, something shifted, it was at a bible study at my uncle's house, he asked me to close out in prayer and my first words were, "I can't do that." He said it again, "just start talking and the Holy Spirit will do the rest." So, I did and before I knew it, I was leading prayer circles and being called to pray at every woman's group I was a part of, and according to people, I was good at it, too. Not tooting my own horn or anything but once you learn a thing, you should try to master that thing.

From there, I began to feel the Holy Spirit pulling at me about ministry, I remember being afraid, confused and shock that God would use a nobody such as me to preach his Word to his people but when the confirmation came on a first Sunday, I heard Him loud and clear and I mean I was slain in the Holy Ghost right in the choir loft. Like Isaiah, my reply was "Here I am Lord send me." And what did I do that for, because it has been a very bumpy road since then but also one, I would not change for the world. Once I was licensed to preach, I talked to my dad and what he said to me about it was the same exact thing my uncle had spoken to me; to just open my mouth and the Holy Ghost do the rest. As things began to unfold, the jealousy and mistreatment follow, and I just knew that the God of all grace surely must've seen all the nonsense I was experiencing inside and outside the church. I mean from the hierarchy and not lay people. The lay people welcomed me with opened arms but my clergy peers, they wanted nothing to do with me, but they tolerated me.

We must understand that the call on one's life doesn't block the darts that come along with that call. It will make you feel depleted and defeated if you're not careful of what you take in. I strongly remember being at a women's conference and when it was time for dinner, all the ministers were at the same table including myself as the reserved sign was labeled for ministers. The leader of the conference came to the table and asked me to remove myself and sit at another table. I was so embarrassed, but you know what, I didn't bother asking why, I simply did what was asked of me. I was surely confused,

Was I not a minister?

I'm licensed like they are, called like they are, and people know who I am. God what's the issue?

God simply answered, "In time daughter, you will surely understand." I never told anyone; little did I know though that my mom overheard the entire thing. She came and pulled me to the side and said, "You are just as good as any one of them; sometimes, jealousy can't help itself and people act out that jealousy and do not even realize it. I heard God clearly say, "AMEN!"

I don't understand why those that have been in ministry for several years think they have the market cornered on God, but God can use the lowest of the lowest and have them do great and mighty things through the leading of the Holy Ghost. I was cast aside by leaders that I held in high esteem and were very friendly with me, I guess if I stayed out of their lane. They may as well have said, "don't come over here where you don't belong." It's a mighty good thing that

God decides where we do and don't belong because people swear that they're our bosses and not God Himself.

Don't get it confused God will get the glory out of your life good, bad or indifferent. He anoints those He wishes and appoints those whom He trusts to do what He's given them too. Let me encourage you as you may be new to ministry or very seasoned, the anointing costs and God will show you those that He's invited to the table to be a witness of how He will bless you to serve His people in and out of season right before their eyes.

DO YOU TRUST GOD FOR REAL?

Do I trust God? Today I can assuredly say that I do, even though it gets very hard sometimes but back then, I had to keep it moving, hoping and praying that all this would work out for my good as His word says. I felt very unappreciated not only by my clergy peers, but at home as well. When people do not understand that you are in partnership with God is a road that you didn't expect to take and that it's not at all something you asked for, you have no control over the vast things you may have to lose yourself from is certainly not a choice you would otherwise make but you gave God a hearty yes to follow Him.

A life in Christ as I am sure you're finding out is not easy, it is not guaranteed that what you believe God for will come to pass. However, what is sure, what God has planned for your life will come to pass but you must trust Him in all things even in the mess you may be making or the mess you're in that is not of your own doing. As I continue to follow God, even to this day, I come across some very negative people, seems like I can't escape the users, naysayers and mind draining people. It takes a lot of faith, obedience and trust in God to suffer in silence, when you really want to pull the covers off their simpleminded behaviors. But "vengeance is mine says the Lord," so, I let God handle their behaviors towards me while I handle my response towards them.

THE NERVE OF THEM ALL

I recall very vividly, when I was ordained as a pastor back in 2020 within Unstoppable Kingdom Ministries in Brockton, MA., people were full of how that happened questions and even if my ordination was legit. I got so tired of trying to explain myself, the Lord very loudly and clearly ordered me to stop that, and that it was Him that chose me and ordained me and didn't matter if people accepted or agreed with it. I'm behooved at the things people do because they may question it, they aren't doing a thing that concerns what they've been given to do but want to question the things others are doing. It is my hope that I am encouraging even one person to not let insecurities of others to not stop them from pursuing what God has already placed inside them from the very beginning.

GROWING IN HIS GRACE

You know every time, I was faced with conflict about who people assumed I was in the Holy Ghost, from the very start, I always felt like I had something to prove to someone. The more I got closer to God and His expectations of me, I began to suffer in silence, meaning, I let God handle the foes that were growing around me, while I learned to grow in grace.

I must admit though, growing in God's grace and suffering in silence is a learned thing, not an automatic one. The road is lonely and tough because there will be days that the Holy Spirit will not let you utter a word to anyone and when he does allow you to discuss it, more than likely it will be with who you least expected. See doing it that way, there will be no bias, only straight truth and it will embrace what you're feeling or tell you where you went wrong, and it will also give you the space to correct it and move forward. Admittedly, growing in His grace was the hardest thing that I have ever had to do. There were times when I was screaming and crying demanding God to move on my behalf, and He was completely silent. I didn't understand how he could let this happen, I mean really! However, the more I complained of the things that were happening to me, the more God reminded that as long as I did that, the longer my assignment was going undone. BLEW MY MIND! And besides, no one can demand God to do anything. He moves on His time, when He feels you have learned the lesson. This sounds exactly like my father, he would punish us for our misbehavior, and we couldn't go outside. And after some time had passed, we would ask if we could go outside and his reply would be "why are you asking me" and me for instance would say you have me grounded, he would then say I do, well why do you think I should let you go outside, and we had to explain what we got from being grounded. I hated that! But I tell you what, I wouldn't commit that crime again.

Growing in his grace means that you may not like everything that you're going through but because of the suffering for Christ that you have experienced, He is going to make sure that you come out better than you went in. I am so much better at this moment in my life, even though the doubt and persecution that I experienced is still happening even as I write the words on this page. But God, that's all I have to say on that. I will continue to do and be what my father has given to me to do and who He has exalted me to be.

Do you think you can be an encourager, now that you've gone through your experience?

Being an encourager means you have the capacity to weather the storm since you have come through it yourself. But it also means that you're able to put yourself in the back and the concerns of others in the front. Your darkest days will now be someone else's hope that they too can come through and be alright. God, He now trusts that because you were once the victim but now the victor, He expects you to handle the person with compassion, honesty, care, confidentiality and to show them mercy. The last thing you want to do is throw salt on someone because of their circumstance or even a sin they may have committed. God could've easily done the same thing to you. However, he doesn't hold anything over our heads or throw it back in our faces, once the storm is over. An encourager is always looking for the good in someone to point out to them; many people, when facing a hard trial in life, to them life looks very bleak and has no meaning.

That is why for me it took God and the others that He was placing in my life to help me see the bigger picture and that life was still worth the living after my husband and partner in life for 27 years wanted a divorce. Lastly being an encourager is like giving your own life a reset, you feel great helping people come out of the despair that they were facing and assisting them to get to Jesus the healing of their fate. Great job if that is you. I pray I am encouraging you even now as you read this book.

What has been learned from all this?

I continue to try to be an example of fighting in silence to all I encounter but it takes confidence in your new self to not allow the actions of other people bother you. The truth is though; people are going to be people and they're going to believe what they want to believe even if the person has changed. I found out the closer I began getting to God, I realized that it didn't matter because they will always hold the bad over your head and completely ignore the changes in you that they see with their very eyes. God is the only person you must prove anything too because He's the one that holds your destiny in His hands. So, learning lessons when you go through various trials and storms, God is testing your ability to grow and discover your own truths. I began to look back on the things that happened and how they affected me, once I gained power over how their actions made me react, is the moment I began to grow as a woman of God and learn to not allow myself to stoop to the level of those that afflicted me.

I gleaned a lot from the bad and good that I've gone through, my relationship with God has brought me all this way and I couldn't imagine life without Him. However, as I stated earlier, what can't be done especially for us as women and women in ministry, we cannot afford to let the silly acts that are committed against us depict how we're going to turn out. It was a long battle getting over being taken for granted or being placed in a lower place than others, but you know what with the grace of God and the power of the Holy Ghost resting inside me, I was able to show them the same love I aways had because I wasn't the aggressor, they were. I kept a smile on my face and even had the courage enough to hug them when I was in their presence. Only God can take you through hurt in that manner, but I did get through it.

The Awakening

Up to this point the chapter has been about the pains of my life and some of the things that passed my way. But now, I want to share what transpired to assist my growth and to get me to the point where I don't react to other people's shortcomings. You too can do the same. You can look at your own storms and glean what you can from them and take control of how you react to people's idiosyncrasies.

I was at one point in my life completely devastated over the things that happened to me in ministry or even in my personal life. I couldn't function in the capacity that God expected of me. I had to come to grips with myself not the others and that is huge. This is where my encouragement to you stems from and not even to say that you're living in some sheltered existence, but it is my hope that this blesses you in some way.

The question is on the table is the very same question God asked me, the question that opened my eyes and dried up every tear I was crying at the time and that question is, am I satisfied with my actions, my living and am I accountable for what I do and how I react to the actions of others. He wanted me to honest about whether I dropped the ball on how I've handled other people, was I always His representative or did my emotions take me over the cliff. When God asked me that, it began my change and redirected me on a path I never dreamed of. I had to start considering everything I allowed myself to get into and the things that others inflicted upon me, I was very careful with my reactions to them. Because remember in (Matthew 25:40), Jesus reminds us that what we did to others, we've also done to Him. I had finally realized that the infraction wasn't about the other person but was a test of my claims that I am on the Lord's side doing what He called me to do, abuse and all, does not change the assignment on my life, nor does it change the call on yours.

The Final Curtain Call; The Healing to Move Forward

As I stated only a few moments ago, all you've experienced as a woman in ministry, it does not change the call on your life but at the same time, there you stand heartbroken and ashamed for what you have experienced. The number one thing you must do, I am sure you know, yes pray! But it's what you pray that matters. I had to shift my prayers with all my broken pieces and pray to God, get this: "LORD MAKE ME BETTER AND NOT BITTER". This prayer opened so many doors and taught me so much about myself, forgiveness and truly living my life out for God and allowing him to be my Lord and Savior. I had to put myself completely in His hands knowing that my breakthrough was only a matter of time. But in the meantime, even if I didn't preach or minister in some capacity, I still engulfed myself in spending much needed time with Him and allowing Him to heal my brokenness and trust that He was in my corner, working things out. Trusting God when you have been so misused doing what He's asked you to do, trusting Him is hard thing but a most necessary thing. See it's all about Romans 8:28, "…**all things work together for the good of those who love God and called according to His purpose."**

That's you right? We'll let the people be them and you continue to be you, the anointed, called and full of the Holy Ghost woman of God.

God bless you and continue to pray for me, as I pray for you.

A Place of Divine Reflection

A Place of Divine Reflection

Tammy Vaughan

Pastor Tammy Vaughan serves as the Senior Pastor of Freedom Christian Center in Burlington, North Carolina. She is a wife, mother, and grandmother of five. Academically, she holds a master's degree in social work and is a Licensed Clinical Social Worker. She is also the CEO of Gracepoint Recovery Services, LLC, where she and her assist youth and adults with mental health and substance abuse issues. Pastor Tammy is a certified Life Coach and CEO of Bhealed for the past ten years; she has coached hundreds of women and men to walk through deep trauma and heal their wounds to have life-changing breakthroughs.

With a passion to help women and men share their stories to impact the world, Pastor Tammy launched the DESTINED TO WIN book series, with seven volumes completed to date inclusive of over 100 authors.

At her core, Pastor Tammy is a servant-leader whose life is anchored in following Jesus Christ. She is deeply committed to helping others maximize their potential and firmly believes everyone deserves the opportunity to live with wholeness, freedom, and purpose.

Her Motto is: To make a great life one must give to others (Winston Churchill)

Contact Pastor Tammy:

Email: destinedwinner2020@gmail.com

Facebook:
https://www.facebook.com/groups/bhealedcoaching/
https://www.facebook.com/groups/winningwithwinners/

Websites: www.destinedtoinspire.com

Called, Equipped, and Empowered: A Journey of a Woman in Ministry
by Pastor Tammy Belle

Introduction: The Call that Changes Everything

God's call on a woman's life is undeniable, powerful, and deeply personal. Whether whispered in a moment of stillness or shouted through a burning desire to serve, the call to ministry is sacred. For women, answering that call can be both exhilarating and challenging. Ministry has long been a domain perceived as male-led, but the Bible is replete with examples of faithful, strong, spirit-filled women who led, prophesied, taught, and ministered.

The call to ministry is a divine invitation that disrupts the ordinary and awakens a holy urgency within. It is not merely a career path or religious obligation—it is a sacred assignment from God that redefines identity, purpose, and direction. When a woman hears and responds to this call, everything changes. Priorities shift, comfort zones are stretched, and personal ambitions are surrendered for a greater cause. It is the moment when God says, "I have chosen you," and suddenly, life becomes less about self and more about service.

Like Moses at the burning bush, or Mary receiving the angel's message, the call may come unexpectedly but carries eternal weight. It speaks to the deepest parts of us, igniting passion and provoking reverence. For many women, this call may challenge cultural norms or religious traditions, but it cannot be silenced by resistance or fear. It carries with it the authority of heaven and the empowerment of the Holy Spirit. The call is not based on perfection, but on God's purpose. It demands faith, sacrifice, and resilience, yet offers unparalleled fulfillment in walking out God's will. It is a call to weep with the broken, stand in the gap, proclaim truth, and lead with compassion.

When God calls a woman to ministry, it is a transformative summon that changes not only her life—but the lives of everyone she is called to reach. It is the beginning of a journey that marks her with eternal significance.

"The Lord gives the word; the women who announce the news are a great host."

Psalm 68:11, ESV

This verse is not just a poetic declaration—it is a divine validation of women called to carry the Gospel. In this chapter, we will explore the biblical foundations for women in ministry, share reflections from the field, address the unique challenges women face, and end with an encouraging word to help you keep going.

A Biblical Foundation for Women in Ministry

From the beginning, God demonstrated that women have a purpose in His redemptive work.

Eve was not an afterthought—she was created to partner with Adam in stewarding creation (Genesis 2:18). **Deborah**, a prophetess and judge (Judges 4-5), led Israel with wisdom and courage. **Esther** risked her life to save her people (Esther 4:14). **Mary**, the mother of Jesus, surrendered to God's plan with the words, *"Let it be to me according to your Word."* (Luke 1:38).

In the New Testament, Jesus broke cultural norms to affirm women:

- He spoke with the Samaritan woman and revealed Himself as the Messiah (John 4).

- Mary Magdalene was the first to see the resurrected Christ and was commissioned to tell the disciples (John 20:17–18).

- Priscilla, alongside Aquila, taught Apollos more accurately the way of God (Acts 18:26).

Paul acknowledged the leadership of women like **Phoebe**, a deacon (Romans 16:1), and **Junia**, noted among the apostles (Romans 16:7).

Jesus' ministry was radically inclusive, especially in His treatment of women. In a culture that often silenced or marginalized them, Jesus elevated women, affirmed their worth, and included them in His work. He spoke directly to women, taught them alongside men, and entrusted them with spiritual truths. So, the next time someone questions your call, remind them:

God called women then—and He still calls us now.

Answering the Call: Your "Yes" Matters

Your "yes" to God is not just a step—it is a leap into a lifelong adventure. Like Mary, you may not know all the details, but your obedience unlocks divine purpose. Saying yes often means saying no to comfort, applause, and predictability. Ministry demands resilience. It requires dying to self, surrendering ambitions, and trusting God to be your provision and protector.

"And I heard the voice of the Lord saying, 'Whom shall I send, and who will go for us?' Then I said, 'Here am I!' Send me.'"

Isaiah 6:8

The moment you say yes, heaven begins to align resources, mentors, and opportunities to prepare you. But be aware warfare often follows the call.

God does not wait for perfection—He looks for obedience. When you say "yes" to His call, you align yourself with divine purpose. Your "yes" may not feel grand, but in God's hands, it can shift atmospheres, break chains, and ignite healing in others. Esther's "yes" saved a nation. Mary's "yes" birthed the Savior. Your willingness today could be the catalyst for someone else's breakthrough tomorrow. You may feel unqualified, but God equips those He calls. Even in fear or uncertainty, your obedience declares, "Here I am, Lord. Use me." Heaven moves when faith meets surrender.

So, do not underestimate the power of your "yes." It does not have to be loud—it just has to be true. In your simple surrender, God does extraordinary things. Say "yes," and watch Him do what only He can. Jesus' ministry was radically inclusive, especially in His treatment of women. In a culture that often silenced or marginalized them, Jesus elevated women, affirmed their worth, and included them in His work. He spoke directly to women, taught them alongside men, and entrusted them with spiritual truths.

One profound example is **Mary of Bethany**, who sat at His feet as a disciple (Luke 10:39)—a position traditionally reserved for male learners. Jesus defended her choice, declaring she had chosen "the better part." He also revealed His identity as the Messiah first to the **Samaritan woman at the well** (John 4:26), who then became one of the earliest evangelists, bringing her entire town to hear Him. After the resurrection, Jesus appeared first to **Mary Magdalene** and appointed her to carry the message of His victory to the apostles (John 20:17). In doing so, He made a woman the first witness of the Gospel. These moments were not accidental; they were intentional acts of empowerment, demonstrating that Jesus values, calls, and uses women in ministry.

Or me, the girl who said YES but…

The Weight and Wonder of the Work

Ministry is a beautiful burden. There's joy in seeing lives transformed, prayers answered, and truth preached. But there's also heartache in rejection, spiritual attacks, and seasons of invisibility. Paul wrote,

> *"We are hard pressed on every side but not crushed; perplexed, but not in despair."*
>
> **2 Corinthians 4:8**

Women in ministry often face additional challenges:

- **Being underestimated**: Your qualifications may be questioned despite your fruitfulness.

- **Navigating gender bias**: Some traditions still resist women in leadership.

- **Balancing family and ministry**: Guilt and burnout can be constant battles.

- **Feeling alone**: Especially if you are one of the few women leaders in your context.

But remember, your labor is not in vain (1 Corinthians 15:58). Every sermon preached, prayer whispered, and soul nurtured matters deeply to God.

Being a woman preacher carries both a sacred weight and a breathtaking wonder. The weight comes from knowing that every message delivered, every soul reached, and every truth declared carries eternal significance. It also comes from navigating expectations, stereotypes, and scrutiny that can sometimes be harsher simply because of gender. There are moments of silence from pulpits where your voice is not welcomed, and moments of resistance from those who question your call. These challenges are real—but they do not outweigh the wonder. The wonder is found in watching hearts soften under the power of God's Word spoken through your lips. It is in seeing someone set free because you dared to preach deliverance. It is in the little girl who sees you standing in authority and begins to dream God-sized dreams for her own life. It is the joy of co-laboring with the Holy Spirit, feeling His power flow through you as you proclaim hope, healing, and salvation.

"How beautiful on the mountains are the feet of those who bring good news."

Isaiah 52:7 (NIV)

Preaching as a woman is not about proving yourself—it is about presenting Christ. It is a privilege and a calling, not a platform for ego but a posture of surrender. There is weight, yes, but oh, the wonder of being entrusted to declare the unsearchable riches of Christ. As a woman preacher, you carry both the burden and the beauty—and by God's grace, you do it well.

Sisterhood and Support

One of the greatest gifts in ministry is the strength found in sisterhood. As women walking out our divine callings, we were never meant to do it alone. Ministry can be isolating at times, but when we link arms with other women of faith, we create a powerful network of encouragement, wisdom, and prayer. Sisterhood in ministry means having someone who understands the weight of the work, the tears behind the podium, and the silent battles fought in prayer. It is the seasoned mentor who reminds you to rest, the peer who celebrates your victories, and the younger sister who draws inspiration from your walk. Together, we share wisdom, laughter, and accountability—forming bonds that are both spiritual and practical.

The early church was built on such connections. Women like **Mary**, **Priscilla**, **Lydia**, and **Phoebe** did not serve in solo; they worked together, supported the apostles, and hosted churches in their homes. Their legacy reminds us that ministry thrives in community.

"And let us consider how we may spur one another on toward love and good deeds."

Hebrews 10:24 (NIV)

In a world that often tries to pit women against each other, true sisterhood chooses unity over competition. It cheers loudly, prays deeply, and loves unconditionally. When women in ministry support one another, we become a force of healing, hope, and holy power. Together, we are stronger—and together, we shine brighter for the Kingdom. Hear me and hear me well………..Isolation is dangerous in ministry. God created us for community—especially as women who lead. Here are some strategies I encourage you to use while serving as a woman in ministry.

- **Seek out other women in ministry**: Do not compete, collaborate.
- **Mentor and be mentored**: There's wisdom in shared stories.
- **Be vulnerable**: Share your struggles with safe sisters.
- **Celebrate others**: Their win is not your loss.

"Two are better than one... If either of them falls down, one can help the other up."

Ecclesiastes 4:9–10

Surround yourself with women who speak life, offer wise counsel, and pray fervently. Ministry is a team effort, not a solo mission.

The Oil and the Overflow

In ministry, especially as a woman, it is essential to understand the difference between the oil and the overflow. The oil represents the anointing—the sacred empowerment from God that enables us to preach, teach, lead, and serve effectively. But the overflow is what pours out after we have been filled through intimacy with God. You cannot serve others from an empty vessel. Without the oil, our efforts are dry. Without the overflow, burnout is inevitable. As women in ministry, we often give so much: our time, energy, counsel, and prayers. We pour and pour until we are drained and then wonder why joy and peace feel far away. That is why maintaining our personal altar is not optional, it is vital. Time in worship, the Word, and rest is how the oil is replenished.

Like the widow in chapter 4 of 2 Kings, who poured from a small jar of oil and filled many vessels, our obedience creates room for miracles. But note: the oil only flowed as long as there were empty vessels to receive. We must be wise enough to know when to pause, when to refill, and when to allow God to pour into us again.

> *"But my horn you have exalted like that of a wild ox; fine oils have been poured on me."*
>
> **Psalm 92:10 (NIV)**

Your anointing is precious. Guard it. Nurture it. And when you minister, let it be from the overflow—not striving, but spilling over from a well that has been filled by God.

"Here are some key strategies I encourage you to embrace as you walk faithfully in ministry. These practices are designed to help you stay grounded, nurture your spiritual health, and lead others with wisdom, grace, and integrity. As you serve, remember that your effectiveness in ministry flows from your connection with God and your commitment to grow, love, and lead with a servant's heart."

Your public ministry must be fueled by private devotion. You cannot pour from an empty cup.

- **Stay in the Word**: Scripture is your sword and sustenance.
- **Guard your prayer life**: It is the lifeline of your call.
- **Sabbath is sacred**: Rest is resistance against burnout.
- **Check your motives**: Serve from love, not from applause.

Like the wise virgins in Matthew 25, keep your oil filled. Do not let the demands of ministry drain your intimacy with God.

You were called to minister *with* God, not just *for* Him.

Fruit That Remains

One of the most profound promises of ministry is found in the assurance that our labor is not in vain—that the fruit we bear will remain. For women in ministry, this truth is both a comfort and a challenge. The work we do may sometimes feel invisible or undervalued, but God sees every seed sown, every prayer whispered, and every life touched.

Jesus said,

> **"My Father's glory is shown by this: that you bear much fruit, proving you are my disciples."**
>
> **John 15:8, NLT**

As women called to ministry, our fruit might look different in form and timing, but it is equally vital. Whether it is a transformed heart, a restored family, or a renewed community, the impact of your ministry endures. Sometimes, we measure success by immediate results, but God's kingdom operates on a timeline beyond our sight. The encouragement you offer today may blossom into a ministry tomorrow. The faith you nurture in one woman can ripple into generations.

> *"I have chosen you and appointed you so that you might go and bear fruit that will last."*
>
> **John 15:16 (NIV)**

This promise encourages us to persevere. Your faithful service, your tears, your prayers, and your words carry eternal value. Ministry is not about fleeting applause but about eternal influence. Trust that the fruit you bear as a woman in ministry is planted deeply in the fertile soil of God's grace—and it will remain long after you see the harvest.

Impact in ministry is not measured by likes, titles, or stages. It is seen in lasting fruit.

- **The woman who walked away from abuse.**
- **The teen who found identity in Christ.**
- **The addict who now leads recovery groups.**
- **The leader who was mentored and is now mentoring others.**

Jesus said,

"You did not choose me, but I chose you and appointed you so that you might go and bear fruit— fruit that will last."

John 15:16

When you wonder if it is worth it, look for the fruit. It always tells the truth.

Don't Quit Now: Keep Going

Ministry is a journey filled with highs and lows, moments of joy and seasons of challenge. For women in ministry, the road can sometimes feel especially tough marked by opposition, misunderstanding, exhaustion, and self-doubt.

But if you have felt like giving up, this is the moment to hear God's encouragement:

Don't quit now. Keep going.

The call to ministry is not for the faint of heart. It requires perseverance and resilience. You may face doors closing, voices of discouragement, or the heavy weight of unmet expectations. But remember, God's strength is made perfect in our weakness (2 Corinthians 12:9). When you feel drained, it is an invitation to lean harder on Him, not to walk away from the call.

"Let us not become weary in doing good, for at the proper time we will reap a harvest if we do not give up."

Galatians 6:9 (NIV)

This promise reminds us that the fruit of ministry does not always appear overnight. Sometimes, the seeds you plant today will not sprout until years from now. The lives you have touched, the prayers you have prayed, and the wisdom you have shared are building something eternal—whether you see it yet or not. Consider the stories of biblical women who persevered: Hannah prayed fervently through years of barrenness before Samuel's birth (1 Samuel 1), Ruth chose faithfulness in a foreign land, and Mary, the mother of Jesus, endured the pain of watching her son suffer, yet never wavered in her trust. Your "no quitting" attitude is a testament to your faith and obedience. It also serves as a beacon for others—showing younger women that ministry is a marathon, not a sprint.

Remember, you are not alone. Lean on your sisterhood, pray for renewed strength, and hold tightly to God's Word. When the enemy whispers that you are done, remind yourself who has called you and how faithful He is.

> ***"But those who hope in the Lord will renew their strength. They will soar on wings like eagles; they will run and not grow weary; they will walk and not be faint."***
>
> **Isaiah 40:31 (NIV)**

Keep going. Your journey matters. Your obedience matters. And the harvest ahead is worth every step. There will be days you want to quit. Days when you feel invisible, inadequate, or ignored. Days when the warfare outweighs the wins. But let me remind you:

You are not alone. You are not overlooked.
You are not underqualified.

"Let us not grow weary in doing good, for at the proper time we will reap a harvest if we do not give up."

Galatians 6:9

You were created for such a time as this. You were anointed to carry God's Word. You were chosen to be a light in dark places. When the enemy tries to silence your voice, raise it louder. When fear tells you to sit down, stand taller. When doubt creeps in, declare the promises of God.

Closing Encouragement:

Persevere in Your Divine Calling

As you walk this path of ministry as a woman, remember that you are part of a powerful legacy—women who have gone before you, and women who will follow, all bound together by God's calling and purpose. Your journey will have moments of struggle, doubt, and opposition, but it is also filled with divine appointments, breakthroughs, and joy beyond measure. The road may not always be easy, but it is always worth it. God's Word assures us that He equips those He calls (Hebrews 13:21) and that His grace is sufficient in every season (2 Corinthians 12:9). You do not have to be perfect or have all the answers—just be willing to be used. Your authenticity, your passion, your faithfulness, and your perseverance are what God uses to bring hope, healing, and transformation.

Lean into the strength of the Holy Spirit, embrace the support of your sisters in Christ, and never underestimate the power of your "yes." Every sermon preached, every prayer lifted, every act of service echoes into eternity. The fruit of your labor will remain, even when you cannot see it now. So, hold fast, dear sister. Keep pressing forward with courage and confidence. Your ministry is not only needed, it is vital. The world needs your voice, your love, and your boldness. Keep shining, keep serving, and above all, keep trusting the One who called you by name.

"Be strong and courageous. Do not be afraid; do not be discouraged, for the Lord your God will be with you wherever you go."

Joshua 1:9 (NIV)

Your calling is sacred. Your impact is eternal. Keep going — the best is yet to come. Always remember this scripture **Psalm 46:5** as you continue on your journey.

> **"God is within her, she will not fall; God will help her at break of day."**

Psalm 46:5 (NIV)

As a woman called to preach the Gospel, Psalm 46:5 is a divine assurance that **you are not standing alone in your calling**. God Himself is within you—empowering your voice, strengthening your steps, and guiding your heart. When challenges come, when your authority is questioned, or when the weight of ministry feels heavy, remember this: **you will not fall**, because the One who called you is also the One who holds you. At the break of day—just when it feels darkest—**God's help will rise**, faithful and on time. Keep preaching, keep pressing, and keep standing. Your calling is valid, your voice is needed, and your presence in the pulpit is **divinely backed**.

You are not just a preacher—you are a vessel of God's power, and **He is within you, and YOU will NOT fail!**

~**Keep Going**

A Place of Divine Reflection

A Place of Divine Reflection

A Place of Divine Reflection

A Place of Divine Reflection

www.ingramcontent.com/pod-product-compliance
Lightning Source LLC
Chambersburg PA
CBHW050644160426
43194CB00010B/1798